"You will get swept along on this darkly humorous journey from the depths of super-stuck to the dizzying heights of superhero. A must read for any parent of a special kid who knows deep down they are capable of much more than their dim prognosis. I have had the pleasure of guiding Rosemary and her mother to success, and I am so proud of them both! Go Team Rosemary!"

Steven R. Wertz, M.Div., BCBA,
Growing Minds Autism Program Director

"A truly inspirational story about a very special little girl overcoming her health and developmental challenges. Learn how her amazing mum unlocked her full potential, by finding the right nutrition and therapies to help her shine."

Lucinda Miller, Family Naturopath,
Founder of Nature Doc Clinic,
Author of *The Good Stuff*

"This book will show you how to launch your child from struggling to thriving in school."

David Newman, Speech and Language Pathologist,
Author of *Working Memory Activities* and *Inference Activities*

"It is so inspiring to hear how far this young lady has come. I am very honoured that I was part of this incredible journey. I support all the super kids and super parents out there, both in heart and spirit, and pray that you all achieve your dreams!"

Tali F. Berman, Autism Specialist,
Author of *Play to Grow*

Special Kid *to* Super Kid

OVERCOMING LEARNING DISABILITY, LANGUAGE DELAY, AND AUTISM

*Discover the 10 Secrets of
Unleashing Your Child's Superpowers*

RUTHANGELA BERNADETTE

Printed in the United States of America
Published by Author Academy Elite
PO Box 43, Powell, OH 43035
www.AuthorAcademyElite.com

This book is not intended as a substitute for the medical advice of physicians. The reader should regularly consult a physician in matters relating to their own or their child's health, and particularly with respect to any symptoms that may requrie diagnosis or medical attention. The information in this book is not meant to replace the advice of a qualified physician.

I have tried to recreate events and conversations from my memories of them, and accept that the fog of time may have clouded the accuracy of my recollections.

In order to maintain their anonymity, I have, in some instances, changed people's names, identifying characteristics and details.

The Son-Rise Program® is a registered trademark of Barry Neil Kaufman and Susan Marie Kaufman. The Autism Treatment Center of America® is a trademark of the Option Institute and Fellowship. The Son-Rise Program Developmental Model Copyright © 2007 by William Hogan and Bryn Kaufman Hogan.

Library of Congress Control Number: 2019919783
ISBN: 978-1-64746-062-4 (paperback)
ISBN: 978-1-64746-063-1 (hardback)
ISBN: 978-1-64746-064-8 (ebook)
Available in paperback, hardback, e-book, and audiobook.

To my precious daughter, Rosemary.

You are the most beautiful person I have ever met. Beautiful on the outside. Beautiful on the inside. Not only are you are the most loyal, loving, trusting person I have ever had the privilege of knowing, you have the most touching and graceful humility about how far you have come and how much you have achieved.

It is because of you that I am a better person. You have taught me to never give up on my dreams, even when the rest of the world was telling me to stop.

I only hope that someday I might become half the person that you are.

My love forever,

Mum x

Contents

Part III: The Success

Part IV: The Secrets

PART I

The Situation

CHAPTER 1

I Thought This Day Would Never Come

I stand at the school gates, watching.

They come out in their twos and threes, laughing and jostling one another. I catch a glimpse of my eleven-year-old daughter's beautiful curls amid the chatter of girls as they huddle and listen to what she is saying, then collapse into a heap of adolescent giggles.

'Afternoon, girls.'

'Hi, Rosangela.', They chorus.

'Ready to go, love?'

My daughter turns and waves to her friends.

'Bye! See you tomorrow.'

We walk together to the car, enjoying the afternoon sunshine. Kids whizz past on bikes calling to my daughter as they go.

'Bye, Rosemary!'

My daughter calls back to them as we get into the car.

I turn and look at my daughter for a moment. My heart bursts with pride. She thrives in school, has friends, goes to parties, and sleepovers. She is, in essence, a typical eleven-year-old girl. I thought this day would never come. Why? Because Rosemary was diagnosed with autism, learning disability, and language delay.

It seems a lifetime ago when the A-word was first uttered. But it wasn't uttered, it wasn't even spoken. It was roared.

'And she's autistic!', yelled the childminder.

My jaw dropped. Did she really shout after me in the street that my beautiful baby daughter was autistic? Talk about a low blow, saying anything to win an argument.

Placing my toddler in Jean's care had been a stroke of genius, in my opinion. Rosemary had been suffering from a lot of high temperatures, ear infections, and throat infections, week in and week out, not to mention feeding problems, colic, and general fussiness.

I had been summoned to the CEO's office one morning. 'Now I know you are a single mother, and your family isn't close by, but your child appears to be sick an awful lot, and you have been taking a considerable amount of time off work to care for her.'

He paused while he picked at a piece of skin on his face, then flicked it away with his fingers.

Well, that's hygienic.

He continued.

'We appreciate you are working from home, nights, weekends sometimes, I mean you're always on top of things, and we're happy with the quality of your work. We just need to see you about the office more often. You're going to have to make alternative arrangements when your child is sick.'

He paused again.

So much for last week's little speech about work-life balance then.

'Of course, you know I don't have any kids of my own but . . .'

No shit Nigel.

'. . . but working from home is just not the same Ruthangela. I'm sure you understand.'

'Yes, I understand.'

Twat!

Annoyingly, he was right. Rosemary was sick a lot. My one-year-old daughter was enrolled in a large nursery, about a hundred children or so. No doubt that was the problem, I mused. A hundred kids with, say, on average, one school-age sibling each. That's . . . let me see . . . about twenty zillion bugs bouncing off the nursery walls at any given time? Maybe she should go to a childminder with only a couple of kids on her books. Fewer bugs are hanging around there for sure. She had just settled at her nursery; the staff loved her, and so did the other kids. The last thing I wanted to do was take her out of there, but what's a mother to do?

I had a brainwave. I would enrol her half the week with a childminder, and the other half she would stay in the larger nursery. In my reckoning, Rosemary then would only be exposed to half the number of germs with such an arrangement. Then when her little immune system had a chance to toughen up a bit, I would move her back full time into the big nursery she so loved. Genius! I found Jean, who lived right across the road from the big nursery, and she had a vacancy. She was a friendly lady, very polite, and she loved children. But, she had a quality about her that creeped me out. She had a queasy grin. Each time she cracked a smile, my bile would rise, and I found myself swallowing hard.

Oh, God, no! She's smiling again. Don't say anything funny for God's sake!

'Erm, terrible weather we're having, isn't it Jean? Jean?'

Oh yeah, I almost forgot, her psychopathic smile wasn't the only thing off about the woman. That was problem number one, but problem number two was worse. Problem number two was her eyes. The left turned out, and the right turned in. Just exactly who she was looking at was entirely debatable.

Actually, I think she is looking at me.

'Jean? The rain this morning?'

'Yes dear, didn't the heavens just open?'

Oh, she's closer now. That's easier, yeah, it was me she was talking to, just as long as she doesn't smile again.

I admonished myself for being hard on her. After all, she was just a nice old dear who loved kids. Still, I didn't look forward to drop-offs and collections, keeping conversations as short as I could. I struggled to listen to her without frantically looking around to see who on earth she was talking to.

Yes, it is you she is talking to, not someone behind you.

Lionel Richie's soulful lyrics entered my thoughts. "Hello? Is it me you're looking for?"[1]

Oh, God, not that bloody song again! Just take another breath, make your excuses, and get out of here before you hurl.

Yep, I'm ashamed to admit it, but when I'm nervous, my brain whisks me off to a magical place, a nicer place where a choice musical piece from my eclectic tastes or a television show from my childhood plays in a loop. I can only guess that my brain forces me to temporarily enter this parallel universe to save myself from having to deal with unpleasant feelings. It's been like this for as long as I can remember, and my subconscious choice of song is, more often than not, decidedly Freudian.

A few weeks back, the young rookie sales rep turned up at the offices for what he believed would be a counselling meeting. The rest of us, however, knew that this was code for firing someone instead. The poor guy, he was only a young lad, pacing around the office in his well-pressed green suit and polished shoes. He tried his best to make it look like he was nonchalantly hanging about the place rather than being unsure where he should sit—or what to do with himself in general. An uneasy silence descended upon the office as Austin desperately tried to look busy on his phone, "chasing up a few new leads," while casting furtive glances towards the CEO's closed door, checking his watch, and tugging at his overly starched collar. I could stand it no longer. I stood up. 'Right, my turn to make the tea. Who's having?' I gathered up the tea tray and mugs.

'Austin? Are you having a cuppa? Milk and two sugars, isn't it?'

He nodded.

Oh, God, get me out of here!

Then in my own truly unfiltered style like only I could muster, I flounced out of the office towards the kitchen, singing Dusty Springfield's, "I Just Don't Know What to Do With Myself"[2].

It's probably got a name, this problem of mine. Something like Musical Displacement Syndrome or Reality Avoidance Phenomenon. Yeah, something like that. Probably. I'm sure I'm not the only one.

What? I *am* the only one? Bloody hell!

Back at the childminders, this new arrangement of spending half of the week with Jean had, in theory, been working well. Except, this lady was putting pressure on me to remove my daughter from the big nursery and into her care full time instead. I was reticent. Childminders get sick with no notice. Childminders book last minute holidays and change careers on a whim. Lord knew my life was stressful enough without having to juggle sporadic childcare arrangements. And anyway, this had always been just a temporary thing until my child's immune system was strong enough to return her to the big nursery full time.

A couple of weeks later, when I collected Rosemary from Jean's house, another mother arrived as we were leaving.

She greeted Othermum as I left.

'Evening, Mrs. Chivers!'

'Hi, Jean. Is little George ready?'

'So, are you happy with Rosemary's care to date Miss Bernadette?' she enquired after me.

I whirled around, startled. We had already said our goodbyes, and I was already out on the street. Why on earth was she asking me this now?

'Erm, well, yes . . . I think that . . .'

'So, Rosemary is going to do the full week next week then?' she asked.

'Erm, what?'

'Rosemary is starting full time with me on Monday then?'

'Huh? I never said anything about . . .'

'I turned down business today because I was expecting your child to come on full time with me. It's been two months now.'

'But Jean, little George has been full time with you for the past . . .' interjected Othermum.

'Actually, I'm happy with her part-time arrangements as they stand', I said.

'That's not what we agreed!'

'Agreed what?' Othermum looked lost.

'Jean, we had no such agreement.' I maintained.

'Oh, yes, we did!'

'Please don't raise your voice in front of Rosemary like that. You'll scare her.'

Jean's hands shot to her hips. She was not a happy bunny.

'Right, well, in that case, if you're going to mess me about like that, you can just go!'

'What?'

'Who? Me?'

"Hello? Is it me you're looking for?"

'No, you!'

'Why me?'

'She means me', I explained. 'I'll go.'

I started towards the car, furious, Rosemary on my hip.

'If this is the way you treat your customers, Jean, then perhaps it's best we part company sooner rather than later.'

'Fine!', she roared.

Rosemary's bottom lip started to tremble.

'It's okay, honey, let's just get in the car', I whispered as I picked her up and started towards my car fumbling frantically with the keys, hands shaking.

'And she's autistic!', she yelled down the street after us.

I stopped dead. Who was she talking to? Me? I couldn't be sure. But it was me she was angry with, not the other mother. She must have been talking about Rosemary! My face burned.

I struggled to get my distressed child into her car seat and could overhear the conversation continuing.

'In all the time you've minded George for me, Jean, you never once said anything about him having any issues . . .'

'No, no, George isn't the autistic one Mrs. Chivers . . .'

How on earth could anyone stoop so low as to shout such a disgraceful thing at a mother and child in the street? I muttered to myself as I drove off. Despicable. Yes, Rosemary was a different kind of child. Not backward, not weird, just different. She didn't like too much noise or joining in at circle time with the other kids. But autistic? Give me a break! All kids are repetitive sometimes; that's how they learn!

I drove on, my jaw set in a tight line. If she really thinks Rosemary is autistic, then why did she just throw an autistic toddler out on the street like that? I was absolutely fuming, but I had neither the time nor the luxury to let myself wallow. I was a single mother who worked full time. I had responsibilities, and my daughter came first.

Luckily, the big nursery was delighted to have Rosemary back full-time. The next day, with childcare arrangements sorted and my feelings having had time to settle, I calmly picked up the phone and reported Jean to Ofsted.

If your name is Jean and you're an ex-childminder with a squint, a hot temper, and a serial killer's smile, yes, I was the one who called Ofsted. And yes, you did deserve it, you cross-eyed old bint.

Yet her outburst in the street preyed on my mind. There was no denying that Rosemary was a unique child. A couple of weeks before, I had given her a pen and paper to play with, and she was happily producing some wonderful drawings when she gripped the pen tightly and tensed up her whole body and face for a few seconds. It appeared she did this out of pure excitement, but autistic? Expressionless, speaking in a monotone, lining toys up? Never!

A staff member at the nursery said that she thought Rosemary's speech was a little delayed and wondered if I might have this checked out. When I spoke to her more qualified colleague about this, she dismissed her suggestion as being utter tosh and said that there were other children in the nursery whose speech was less advanced than Rosemary's, and she had no concerns about them either. So I left it. The health visitor did warn me that because Rosemary had been premature, she would be late with her milestones, it was to be expected, and nothing to worry about.

But autistic? No way!

Yet another worry that refused to go away was how often Rosemary was getting sick.

CHAPTER 2

She's Taking Antibiotics— She'll Be Fine

In the hospital, recovering from my C-section, I tried my level best to breastfeed her, but I just couldn't manage it no matter how hard I tried. I felt like such a failure. I really wanted to breastfeed, but Rosemary was getting hungry, and I couldn't help her, so a decision had to be made. 'I bottle fed all four of my boys', said the nurse one fraught evening after another failed attempt to feed. 'And they're all six-foot rugby players now.' That was what I needed to hear. Bottle-fed, she was. It wasn't my wish for her, but it was the best I could do. She was starving. Boy, did she guzzle that first bottle, then fall fast asleep. It was such a weird feeling. I had just given life to another human being, and I felt totally useless. No doubt, I felt this way because of my new mother hormones, I rationalised to myself. "Keep calm and carry on"[3], as they say.

Back home some months later, it was becoming apparent that Rosemary was taking too long to have her bottle, and she was getting fractious, curling up into a ball and squealing. The pieces of the puzzle began to fall into place—my baby had colic. No matter how long I spent getting her wind up, her tummy sill hurt, and when she was uncomfortable, she was hard to pacify. Travelling in the car used to soothe her, so I spent hours driving around the motorway with her in her car seat. I knew every inch of that motorway in detail. When the weather was good, I took her out for long walks in her pram in the hope that she might settle. One particular day, when she was squealing in pain, as I pushed her along, I let my huge tears roll down my face. I didn't care who saw me. So, I was relieved when a few days later, following a conversation with the GP, I took the decision to switch her to a milk-free formula, and the colic disappeared overnight. *Overnight!* It was that dramatic.

Click your fingers. Go on, do it.

Click!

That's how quick it was. All her pain and fussiness stopped immediately, just like that.

As she continued to grow, I gradually added cow's milk into her diet, and she seemed fine with it. I put her previous difficulties with formula milk down to her being a colicky baby and thought no more about it. I had no idea at the time that dairy could be a problematic foodstuff for so many kids. I had no appreciation then that the later complete removal of it from her diet would help her so much.

Colic had not been the only issue then. There were more. From only a few months old, Rosemary seemed to get more than her fair share of ear infections. I could tell a couple of days before a new infection took hold, as she would start to look peaky. Her eyes would become sunken, and dark circles would start to form. She put her fingers into her ears, and her temperature soared. Each time I would return home from the doctor's surgery, clutching a prescription for antibiotics.

One morning, when she was about a year old, I knew my baby was unwell. She had a fever and wasn't taking her bottle. There I was, on my own with my first child, with no family anywhere near, and my baby was sick. So, what did I do? I took her to the doctor's surgery and asked for antibiotics. I felt much better when the doctor told me that it was just an ear infection, and it was very common in babies. The antibiotics would clear it up soon enough. Phew! At least it wasn't anything serious. Keep her well hydrated, finish the course of antibiotics, and if I was worried in any way, I could bring her back to the surgery. I went home and gave her the penicillin and nursed my sick child. She was happy if I held her close, and she cried when I put her down in her cot. So, I spent the rest of the day carrying her about, talking, and singing to her. I was glad I had got an early morning doctor's appointment, so then I could give her all three doses of her penicillin on the first day and kick off her recovery properly.

That night, Rosemary slept in her cot beside my bed. I laid beside her, my hand on her back so I could feel the rise and fall of her breathing. '*It's just an ear infection*', I kept telling myself. '*She's taking antibiotics. She'll be fine.*' Exhausted from nursing a sick baby all day, I drifted off to sleep.

As dawn broke, I opened my eyes and looked over at Rosemary. She was sleeping peacefully—time to check for any fever. I reached over to feel if she was hot.

'Oh, my God, no!' Rosemary's tiny body was covered in a rash. Meningitis! I grabbed the phone and called the doctor's 24-hour helpline.

'Hello? Yes, my baby's got a fever and a pink rash all over her body! She was at the doctor's yesterday, and she said it was just an ear infection!'

'Okay, bring her into A&E', the doctor said. 'I'll tell them you are coming. Give her some paracetamol for her fever and try to get some fluids into her.'

I think I managed to throw on some clothes, change Rosemary's nappy, give her some paracetamol and penicillin, and get her strapped into her car seat within the space of five minutes.

When we arrived at the hospital car park, I couldn't get a parking space anywhere near the entrance to A&E and ended up having to park quite some distance away. I scrambled in my purse for change to pay for my parking. Of course, I didn't have enough coins.

I saw a man approaching. 'Excuse me, sorry, b-but could you possibly change a f-five-pound note? This machine only accepts c-c-coins.' I managed to blurt out. He took one look at me. There I was, in my tracksuit, wearing odd shoes, looking like I had got dressed in a matter of seconds (which I had). He smiled, jangled a few coins in his pocket, then fed some coins into the machine and pushed the button.

'There you go!' He winked as the machine spewed out a ticket, and with that, he turned and walked away. I never paid that man back, and I never saw him again.

Rosemary's car seat was one of those contraptions that doubled as a baby carrier, and so heavy! It must have been my marathon training several years before her arrival that I made good use of that day because I picked her up in her carrier, and ran at full pelt to A&E. 'Up on the toes now, ladies, up on the toes!', our trainer used to shout at the end of our training sessions. We always tried to muster up a sprint finish after our long runs. Proud to report I managed a good old sprint most days, but that was years ago. Today I was most definitely up on my toes but had no free arms to slice the air with and no running buddies to chivvy me along.

I burst into A&E and ran over to the Reception Desk. 'Eh, hello. My baby's sick. She has a f-f-fever and a rash!'

I was directed to a cubicle and, within a minute or two, was greeted by a nurse. She would have been in her forties and shared the car park gentleman's laconic demeanour. It was clear she loved babies. She picked Rosemary up, and they smiled at one another. 'Come with me', she said, and off the two of them went on a little trip around A&E, calling on colleagues, as she introduced her cute little companion to them all.

'What have you got, Maggie? Sprained ankle? Look what I've got!', and she would present her new buddy with a flourish, and Rosemary beamed at her new acquaintance.

'Oh, get away with you!', the other nurse retorted.

'Morning, Faye. What have you got there? Look who is looking after me today!', and Rosemary would grin at Faye, right on cue.

This banter went on for a while. It was obvious the nursing staff all got along well. Another thing was obvious—the nurse was not worried about my baby.

My nerves settled while I watched some more. If the nurse was not overly concerned, then I did not need to be either. My breathing started to normalise, and I drank the water the receptionist gave me. The paper cup trembled in my hand. I looked around the A&E department and tried not to worry, staying in the moment, not overthinking. I watched as people came and went, the sounds of young women click-clacking along the corridor in their stilettoes, the smell of coffee from the café. My head was pounding, and I felt faint. It seemed like forever, but, eventually, I received the news.

'Your daughter is allergic to penicillin.'

I looked up at the doctor. My mouth dropped open.

'Is that all?'

'Yes, that's all.'

'Not meningitis?'

'No, not meningitis. Allergic to penicillin.'

'And it's just an ear infection?'

'Just an ear infection.'

17

I exhaled loudly.

'And how is she?'

'She's not bad. You'll need to keep dosing her with paracetamol and ibuprofen to keep her temperature down, and I'll change your prescription now for you.'

He started to write. 'You did the right thing', he carried on. 'You called the right number and brought her in. If something like this happens again, you do the same thing. Okay?'

I nodded. 'My grandmother was allergic to penicillin.'

'Well, there you go, a chip off the old block.' He smiled and handed me the script.

I smiled back. She was going to be just fine.

There were going to be plenty more ear infections after that day. Looking back, it seemed that the poor little mite only had a couple of weeks of good health before another infection got a hold of her.

Surely this was not normal? Rosemary was my first and only baby, so I had no idea what normal was, but my gut told me that something was wrong.

'Babies get sick a lot.' The GP assured me.

'But this often?'

She cocked her head to the side and nodded.

'Ear infections are very common.' she sympathised.

The dash to A&E that morning was not the only one. It wasn't long before I had to make a similar call again.

'My baby has an infection. Her temperature is off the scale! She's red hot!', I said to the doctor's 24-hour helpline.

Another mercy dash to the hospital ensued. Although this time, I was told that she was going to be admitted to a ward immediately upon arrival. This particular hospital dash was through thick snow on Christmas Eve.

'We're going to have to admit her', said the nurse. This nurse was a young girl, friendly enough, but she did not share the previous nurse's laid-back attitude. She had a concerned look on her face, and her voice was serious. When she picked up Rosemary to assess her, she wasn't joking about with the other nurses.

I sat there in my old tracksuit, which any self-respecting mother dons whenever there are copious amounts of vomit/poo/snot/saliva/wee-wee in the vicinity.

I closed my eyes and made a wish. *Please don't let my baby suffer anymore. Give the infection to me instead and let her be okay.*

A few anxious hours passed. After a period of observation and a drip in her arm for hydration, she was considered well enough to be discharged home that night. I could take my baby home for Christmas! Best present ever!

The doctor diagnosed her with an upper respiratory infection. Plenty of fluids and yet another course of antibiotics were prescribed.

Rosemary showed some progress over the next few days, but her condition worsened again. On New Year's Eve, I was advised to bring her straight back to the hospital ward. This time, the hospital dash was made through waterlogged streets. There had been significant snowfall followed by a thaw, and the roads between my house and the hospital were badly flooded, but I got there, baby and car intact. I was becoming a pro at looking after a sick kid now. This time, I had on a respectable pair of jeans, matching trainers, and only a bit of sick down my tee-shirt. I sat at my baby's side as she lay on the bed, drip in her arm. I looked at her lying there in just her nappy, watching for the rise and fall of her chest, and I suddenly felt calm. I made my wish again. *Dear God, if you are listening, please give the illness to me and let Rosemary be okay. She's too little for all this. Please help her.* God must have listened to me because she got the all-clear again and was discharged home in the early hours of New Year's Day. The following day, I started my course of antibiotics for my infection. Well, if you don't ask, you don't get it.

The last hospital run happened when my daughter was four years old, and it was the most frightening by far. Rosemary had a blast, though! There we were, Rosemary with a roaring temperature, dark rings around her sunken eyes, and I with the phone stuck to my ear, speaking with the doctor's 24-hour helpline.

'Yes, she's four. I think she has an ear infection. She's prone to them . . . She gets them a lot. Well, she's got a high temperature, she's burning hot to touch. She keeps putting her fingers in her ears; she's just not well.'

'Bring her down to the GP's Out of Hours surgery, and we'll see her as soon as we can. Now don't panic; just bring her straight down.'

I looked at my poorly little girl. 'I sick mummy. I sick' she said. Bless her. It was the first time she was ever able to tell me that she was unwell.

'Okay, time to go see the doctor, honey. Come on pet, let's get going.'

She was more withdrawn and quiet, not her usual chatty self. I got her into the car, sickie bowl at the ready just in case. I started the engine and floored the accelerator. *I'll get there in five minutes;* I thought to myself just as I approached a spot in the road known for police officers with speed cameras.

The thought came to me just in time. I eased off the gas and hit the brakes before I rounded the corner. 'Good morning, officer!' I waved out of the open window. He nodded a terse 'Good morning.' I turned right and put my foot to the floor again. I got there in four minutes, feeling like Winston Wolf.

The thing I hate about doctors' waiting rooms is the fact that the moment you leave the waiting area to visit the bathroom is when your name will be called. You can bet your house on it. It's one of those decisions you have to make—should I stay or should I go? If you are lucky, there is a friendly-looking lady who will listen out for your name and tell the doctor that you will be back in a minute. No such luck today. I would have to cross my legs and hope for the best. We were kept waiting for over an hour, but eventually, we were called into the surgery. Rosemary was hot, very hot. The doctor was unsure if it was an ear infection or tonsillitis, and Rosemary wasn't exactly co-operative, being poked in the mouth with a tongue depressor.

'She's just not herself.', I said. 'Usually, if she saw me talking to you, she would be vying for my attention, wouldn't you, Rosemary?'

Nothing.

'Rosemary?'

Rosemary's body went floppy. Then she collapsed.

'Rosemary? Rosemary!' She wasn't responding.

'Let's get her up on the bed', the doctor said, putting an oxygen mask over her face. Rosemary opened her eyes just a slit.

'Rosemary? Rosemary?'

She opened her eyes a little more.

'Mummy . . .'

'Are you okay my darling?'

'Mummy . . .'

The doctor ran to the phone and dialled 999.

'Right, the ambulance is coming.' she said. 'She needs to go to A&E to be checked out.'

'Oh, my poor baby!' I held her close.

It was only a minute or two until the paramedics arrived. We were already in a small village hospital, but she needed transferring to A&E, which was a few miles away. The doctor began to brief the two paramedics on the situation.

'And she's allergic to penicillin!', I interjected a little too loudly.

The first paramedic introduced himself to me.

'Hi, I'm Mike', he said. 'It will take us a while to get Rosemary settled in the ambulance before we take off, so you might as well get a head start in your car, okay?'

'Yes, I'll get the car ready. I need to go to the b-bathroom first, though. Alright, see you there.'

And all you can think of is going to the bloody loo?

I emerged from the bathroom only to have to stop abruptly as the two paramedics rushed past me with my little girl on the gurney. I could hear Mike communicating with the hospital as they hurried past 'Yes, we're on our way. Yes, she lost consciousness again . . . That's right, two episodes . . . She's four years old . . .'

My legs gave way underneath me, and I stumbled against the wall.

It's just the usual drill. We go to the hospital; she gets checked over and then we go home. Breathe.

I suppose four years of caring for a sickly child must have helped me remain calm under pressure. I got into the car, talked to myself, and pulled out of the car park. I had a good head start on the ambulance; they hadn't taken off yet.

Okay, Ruthangela, indicate left, and off we go. Now we're driving . . . we're driving. All good. Put the radio on, that's a good idea.

"If you like pina coladas, and getting caught in the rain".[4]

Admittedly this wasn't the most appropriate of tracks for the situation I was in, but it was a much-needed distraction. I needed something to divert my mind, and a really annoying song from the seventies seemed to fit the bill, so I sang along badly.

It's probably just a convulsion Ruthangela. Into the hospital, a bit of observation, and then home in time for Coronation Street, that'll be it.

I was on the motorway now, and I was going pretty damn fast.

"If you're not into yoga if you have half a brain".

If it were serious, the ambulance would have its sirens on, wouldn't it? And you're still in front of the ambulance, aren't you?

My singing volume increased as did the speedometer.

"If you like pina coladas, and getting caught in the rain".

And do you hear any sirens Ruthangela?, No, you don't! That's because Rosemary is doing just fine. These things happen all the . . .

The ambulance screamed past at breakneck speed, sirens blaring.

Frantic wasn't the word.

Somehow, I managed to stay in control of the car and arrive at the hospital without crashing into anything. I got to A&E and was ushered into a cubicle by myself. I waited, visibly shaking. A nurse arrived and introduced herself and clarified a few details on her admissions form. She was joined a few minutes later by the largest doctor I have ever seen in my life. This guy was about six foot six, and so wide! He spoke with a heavy African accent, and when he smiled, he had the most enormous mouth, and two gold teeth.

I could hear bustling outside. The curtain scraped back. It was Rosemary and the two paramedics.

'Good morning. We have a VIP with us today. This is Princess Rosemary. Princess Rosemary is four years old. She likes Barbies, her favourite colour is pink, and she thinks ambulances are bumpy.'

I almost collapsed on the spot with relief. *Someone must have felt alright in the ambulance then!*

'Are you really a princess?', gasped the nurse.

The little mite nodded slowly and smiled from her gurney.

'And Princess Rosemary, can you tell me where it hurts?', asked the doctor.

'I sick.'

'Yes, I know Princess Rosemary. Where are you sick?'

'I sick.'

The paramedics settled her on the bed and prepared to leave. 'Sorry about the sirens earlier. I didn't want to scare you, but it helps to get through the traffic. Did you see me give you the thumbs up as we passed you?'

No, I bloody well did not!

'Sorry, didn't notice', I managed to whisper.

The medical staff went about their business getting blood and urine samples, taking her temperature, setting up a drip, then leaving us alone while they awaited the test results.

Rosemary laid there, barely moving. Despite her charming conversation in the ambulance earlier, she had had a third syncopal episode en route. She was withdrawn and quiet, *too bloody quiet.* I squeezed her hand. Have you ever willed your kid to be naughty? I did that day. I wanted my impish little girl back. I willed it so hard, but nothing. A few hours passed, and as the wall clock ticked, I looked at my girl. She was such a beautiful child—porcelain doll skin, large pale blue eyes, extraordinarily long eyelashes, and a little rosebud mouth. She had the most gorgeous curly hair, and her face enjoyed a sprinkling of sun-kissed freckles in the summer months. What wasn't there to love? We didn't speak. I just held her hand and thought about how lovely she was on the inside, too. She had the most adorable personality. A bit cheeky and full of mischief, but loyal and trusting. She only ever saw the good in people, even when some kids weren't being kind to her. If only she had her own little best friend. She would make such a good friend, but for some reason, some kids didn't quite take to her as much as others. *What a waste!* I thought—*their loss.*

Rosemary was at her best with me but at her worst in a large group, particularly groups of children, like in nursery. There was just something about that environment that seemed to push all the wrong buttons for her. At times, she became so distressed that her behaviour could get challenging for the nursery staff.

Of late, I had been getting more and more phone calls from the nursery manager complaining that Rosemary was becoming difficult to handle, usually during transition periods. It had been a problem for quite some time, and it was starting to get out of hand. But right then, at that moment, I would have given my right arm for her to act like a spoiled brat. Oh, if only she would just do something naughty, then I would know she was going to be alright! Where had my naughty girl gone?

I started to feel sorry for myself. I was on my own, and I felt totally helpless. My child was sick, I was beside myself with worry, and I didn't have a clue what to do.

Just then, I caught a mischievous little glint in her eye, just a fleeting look.

Go on! I urged silently. *Go on; you know you want to!* I pretended to fall asleep.

Miss Madam got up, ran over to the sink, turned on the tap, then ran and jumped back on the bed. I pretended to wake up with a start, my hand flew up to my mouth, 'Oh, my goodness, somebody left the tap on!' I got up and turned it off, sat back down, closed my eyes, and started to snore.

Little Miss Mischief got back up, turned the tap on, and poked her fingers up the spout, the water spraying everywhere. She giggled and ran back to the bed.

'A-ha! Caught you!'

Rosemary giggled, thoroughly pleased with her antics. 'Mummy, is the doctor a king?'

'Hmmm, I'm not sure. What do you think?'

'He said he was!'

'Well, he must be then, mustn't he?', I said as I mopped the floor with paper towels.

'He magic, too.'

'Is he really?'

'Yeah, he put the magic medicine in.'

'That's right, he did, didn't he?'

'That's not the same child we brought in this morning!', a voice called out. The curtain scraped back. It was the paramedic, Mike.

'Rob! Come in here and see this!', He called to his colleague.

His colleague joined him. Rosemary was now jumping up and down on the bed.

'That's not Princess Rosemary, is it?'

'It most certainly is!'

'Well, Princess, are you feeling better then?'

'I sick.' She lay back down on the bed again, grinning.

My daughter was discharged home with me later that day. Verdict? Tonsillitis and febrile convulsions. Remedy? Yep, you guessed it, antibiotics.

No, I never got a speeding ticket. And yes, later that night, we snuggled up together in my bed and watched *Coronation Street*.

I looked over at Rosemary; she looked tired out, her head resting on the pillow next to me. Poor thing. Time for sleep. I gently sang to my little bird as I stroked her soft curls. She must be drifting off by now, I thought to myself. I finished the lullaby then turned my attention to the television.

'Mummy?', a tiny voice piped up.

I hit the mute button.

'Yes, darling?'

'What a pina-koala?'

If you're reading this book and you're a police officer, I certainly never broke any speed limit that day or on any other day, for that matter. Thank you for the tireless work you do for the community and have a good day.

That was the last day of my daughter's sickly phase. Up until then, she had infection after infection, bug after bug, antibiotic after antibiotic.

Click your fingers again. Do it.

Click!

As quick as that, my daughter's health entered a new phase from that day onwards. Phase 2: the 'Never-Ever-Gets-Sick' phase. It also lasted four years, and when I say never, I mean *never*—she did not get one single sniffle during that time.

You're probably thinking to yourself, *What a drama queen!* That mother's reaction was completely over the top when her kid was sick. It was only tonsillitis for goodness sake! You could be right, it probably was. You see, "drama queen" comes naturally to me. I do drama queen rather well daaaahhhlings. I'll put it down to treading the boards for twenty years, my luvvies. Being a new mother was a completely different kettle of fish. I had no clue about anything; I didn't know what was normal for a child and what wasn't. But my gut instinct had told me something just wasn't right.

Ask yourself the question, 'How many people do you know whose kid is sick on average two weeks in every month?' If you're a parent of a kid on the spectrum, you are probably shouting, 'That's my kid!' Or perhaps you have experienced the other side of the coin, the never-ever-gets-sick kid. Well, my daughter enjoyed both phases, one right after the other. It was really only when she got to the age of eight that her immune system normalised. Nowadays, typically, she gets a cold and a tummy bug every year, depending on what's doing the rounds at school. She would also have a couple of fleeting maladies now and then, which usually right themselves after plenty of fluids and a good night's sleep. That's about the standard, isn't it?

I was glad to have my cheeky little monkey home with me, tucked up in bed beside me watching our favourite TV programme, and blissfully unaware of what was to come next.

CHAPTER 3

The A-Word

As time went by, Rosemary enjoyed good health, and a stable routine of attending nursery whilst I worked. We were happy, just the two of us. She wasn't getting sick all the time. She loved reading books and singing nursery rhymes with me. We had a tight bond, but something in the back of my mind kept niggling at me—there was something odd about Rosemary. That's when the phone calls to work started.

'Hi, Miss Bernadette? It's Sharon from the nursery here.'

'Is everything alright?'

'Yes, sorry to call you at work.'

'Is Rosemary hurt?'

'No, she's not hurt.'

'Is she sick?'

'No, she's not sick.'

'Thank goodness. It's just that, strictly speaking, personal calls aren't allowed you see . . .'

'Miss Bernadette, do you think you could come and collect Rosemary? She's not herself. She got upset during circle time today.'

'Wha . . . what's wrong?'

'I'm not sure. She was doing great this morning then something inside of her just kind of . . . well . . . snapped.'

I could hear screeching in the background. Surely this wasn't my Rosemary making all that racket?

But it was my daughter, screaming.

I drove like a maniac to the nursery to find a hoarse, red-faced, tear-stained little girl waiting for me. I ran to her and threw my arms around her. She looked petrified.

'Rosemary, what on earth is wrong pet? There now. Mummy's here. Give me a hug. What's wrong, darling?'

Rosemary held me tight. 'Mummy . . . mummy, I want mummy.'

'I'm here, darling. What's wrong?'

She looked up at me with her huge eyes. It was as if she was bursting to tell me all about it, tell me what was wrong, and let her all feelings come tumbling out. Her face said so much, but 'I want mummy' was all she managed.

'She's been screaming the place down for the past hour', muttered the nursery manager.

I looked up, but Sharon, the manager, was avoiding eye contact. Rosemary couldn't explain what had upset her so much. Again, I felt like I had failed as a mother in some way. It must be the way I was raising my daughter, working full time, having her spend long days in some nursery when she just needed her mummy. Why else would my child be behaving so disgracefully? I drove her home; my mind was racing. By the time we got there, Rosemary acted as if nothing had happened. She sat down and started playing with her Barbies in the living room. She seemed content. So what had caused all the ruckus earlier?

From then on, things went from bad to worse. As the months went by, the phone calls kept coming.

Ring! Ring!

'Rosemary is distressed. Can you come and get her, please?'

Ring! Ring!

'Rosemary is crying for her mummy. She really is beside herself. Are you able to leave work early?'

Ring! Ring!

'I'm afraid Rosemary has been very naughty this morning, can you collect her early today, please?'

Ring! Ring!

'Can you come and get Rosemary, please? My staff needs a break from her.'

And I need a break from your constant moaning, Sharon dear.

Rosemary had started displaying some unusual habits. I had always encouraged her to change out of her day clothes into her pyjamas when she got home to save on laundry. She seemed to like this daily ritual.

'Hi, Rosemary darling. Time to go home, pet.'

'Change jammies, mummy?'

'Yes, of course, you can.'

'Change jammies, mummy?'

'Yes, you can pet, when we get home.'

As I was pulling her seatbelt around her in the car, she piped up.

'But I change jammies?'

'Yes, dear.'

She was peeling her jumper off as she walked through the front door.

Now in her comfortable pyjamas, she settled down to play with her Barbies. Rosemary loved Barbies. She had over fifty Barbie dolls and all the accessories. My house was bursting to the seams with Barbie stuff. The nursery had even gone shopping and bought a ton of Barbie toys just for her to play with. They must have spent a fortune. The money went to good use, though, as Rosemary spent most of her time at nursery playing with her special toys and didn't interact as much with the other children as they would have liked.

If I were to die and be reincarnated, I would come back to this earth as Barbie. I would wear cutting edge fashion, with matching handbags and six-inch heels. I would drive a pink convertible VW Beetle/SUV/motorbike/jet-ski. I would also have the pleasure of travelling in my own private jet, cruise ship, and bespoke RV, complete with a barbecue set and pull-out jacuzzi. I would spend my evenings with my equally fabulous girlfriends, talking about boys, and texting Ken on my pink phone.

I could be Surgeon Barbie, Air Hostess Barbie, Hairdresser Barbie, depending on my mood on the day. It always fascinated me that I could never find Rehab Barbie, School Run Barbie, or Trailer Park Barbie (beer can, half-smoked fag, and a sink full of dirty dishes sold separately). I would have a healthy BMI of 16.24, my legs would be twice the length of my torso, and my breasts would be so disproportionately large I wouldn't be able to stand upright[5] Well, a girl can dream.

Barbies were all that Rosemary played with at home, day in and day out.

Not only was her choice of toy limited, but her choice of conversation topic was also limited. She asked the same questions all the time, especially when she was travelling in the car. Her grammar would always be perfect when she did this, but not so perfect when she communicated directly with me.

'Why do birds fly, mummy?'

'Because they don't like walking, dear.'

'Where's the rubber duck?'

'In the bath, dear.'

Rosemary had a specific set of questions she would ask me that required a very specific answer. If she did not receive the answer she expected, or if the answer did not come quickly enough, she would have a meltdown.

'Why are zebras stripy?'

'Erm . . .'

'Why are zebras stripy mummy?'

'Hold on a sec, dear; I'm driving the car.' It was rush hour, and I was trying to turn right across a busy road.

'Why are zebras stripy, Mummy?'

'Just give me a minute; I need to concentrate.'

'Mummy, why are zebras stripy?'

'In a minute, pet.'

'Why are zebras stripy, Mummy? Why are zebras stripy?'

Without her required answer, she would wail and kick her legs. She would become frantic, out of control, inconsolable, screaming at the top of her lungs.

'Because the leopard . . . the leopard . . .'

'Mmmuuummmyyy!'

'Because the leopard would be cross if the zebra was spotty, too!'

She would start to settle.

I would be trying desperately to drive safely and console my daughter at the same time.

'It's alright, Rosemary. The leopard would be cross if the zebra were spotty too darling. It's okay.'

'Yes, Mummy, leopard cross.'

And breathe . . .

'Yes, that's right, pet.'

That just wasn't . . . right!

It didn't stop at these repetitive questions. She insisted on wearing the same long-sleeved tee-shirt every day. I did manage to find the same tee-shirt on eBay, but the new fake tee-shirt didn't fool Rosemary. It came a very poor second to the original. She wore the same clothes each day, asked the same questions each day, watched the same Barbie movies each day, and played nonstop with her Barbie dolls. Every. Single. Day.

Okay, okay, I must hold my hands up here and admit it. I am jealous of Barbie. There, I said it. Jealous of the skinny little bitch. Yep, I'm busted. She's just so . . . fabulous! I want to be like her. She never has a bad hair day, never blurts out the wrong thing and puts her foot in it, and she always wakes up looking bloody gorgeous. I love Barbie, and I hate her at the same time. If I'm having a bad day and if the opportunity presents itself to stand on her plastic face, I do it, and I don't care. If you ever find yourself in a similar position, please read my tips below.

Tip # 1:

Do not stand on Barbie's face when your daughter has you in her sights—ever.

Tip # 2:

Do not step on Barbie in your bare feet (too painful).

Tip # 3

Swearing at Barbie doesn't count; she can't hear you.

Tip # 4:

Barbie doesn't hate you, and she's not skinny, gorgeous, and fabulous just to annoy you; honestly, she isn't.

Tip # 5:

Texting Barbie on her pink phone just to tell her she's fat won't make you feel any better about yourself.

Most of our Sunday afternoons consisted primarily of watching Barbie movies and playing with Barbie dolls . . . ad nauseam. I looked forward to going to work on Monday mornings.

The next Monday had been a particularly demanding day. As I drove to the nursery, I prayed the same daily prayer. Maybe if I prayed often enough, he just might give me what I ask for.

Oh, please, let me have one good week, God. Just one good week.

In addition to my daily prayer, on that occasion, I found myself praying for a couple of other things. The first was divine intervention—that some celestial power would in some way help my daughter find inner calm and that her problems at nursery would disappear! *Poof!* The second was that the nursery manager would become otherwise engaged at the same time I arrived each evening to collect my child. I dreaded being called aside by the manager to be told about my daughter's less than ideal behaviour. She had a voice that droned on and on—however, no such luck on both counts. I took a deep breath as I rang the nursery doorbell.

Just think, Ruthangela, it could be worse, it could be her mother!

The manager's mother made a rabid Rottweiler look like a tutu-wearing Chihuahua inhabiting a Swarovski encrusted handbag. I'm sure I spotted one of those in the Barbie Accessories aisle. I crept up the stairs towards the first floor.

'Eh, excuse me, can I have a word?', came the monotones from behind.

I stopped halfway up the stairs. *Busted.*

'Good evening Sharon.'

'Yeah, good evening. Ahem! Little Rosemary has really taken to another child in the nursery, and sometimes she plays really nicely with her. It's just that she follows her around a lot, and it can make the other child a bit uncomfortable, you know.'

'Oh, okay.'

A friend? That's good!

Sharon hesitated.

'And another thing, Rosemary has on occasion hit this other girl.'

I gasped.

'She hit her? Are you sure?'

'Yes, I think it's when she is feeling excited about having a friend of her own to play with. It's like she has so much energy and excitement; she just doesn't know what to do with it.'

'I'm so sorry. I'll speak to Rosemary about this.'

'It's something we really need to nip in the bud, and her mother is very concerned.'

'I can imagine. Yes, I agree. When we get home, we'll talk about it, and she'll get a time out for her troubles of course . . . oh, actually no, have you disciplined her about it yourself?'

'Yes, she was put on the naughty step, and she was made to say sorry.'

'Okay, great, so I don't need to do it again then if you've already done it.'

'And another thing . . .'

There's another thing?

I took a deep breath.

'Lately, when Rosemary has become upset, she's been . . .' Sharon shifted uncomfortably, 'She's been . . . erm . . . taking her clothes off.'

'She's been what?'

'Yeah, it's like she knows it's naughty, and she's only doing it *because* it's naughty.'

'Look, Sharon, I'm so sorry. Really, I am. I don't know what's going on here. This is like nothing I have ever seen. She is as good as gold for me at home. Let me go to her. I'll call you tomorrow.'

What's a mother to do? I needed to get to the bottom of this, but actually hitting another kid? I couldn't let that slide. I didn't smack her, and I certainly wasn't going to let her hit someone.

I went to my daughter's section of the nursery. There she was, happily playing with her Barbie. She heard me come in and looked up with her beautiful pale blue eyes. How could such an angelic-looking little child behave so badly?

Later that night, as I tucked her into her bed, I wondered if she could explain her behaviour to me.

'Rosemary, sweetheart?'

'Yes, mummy?'

'Did you hit Sophie at nursery today?'

There was a pause.

'Erm . . . Can't 'member.'

'Are you sure? Not even a little tap? Sharon told me you did.'

'Oh . . . yeah.'

'You did?'

'Yeah.'

'Why did you do it, darling?'

'I don't know, Mummy.'

'Was it because you were feeling happy?'

'I don't know, Mummy.'

'What about excited? Were you feeling excited?'

'I don't know, Mummy.'

'Do you like Sophie?'

'Yes.'

'How would you feel if Sophie hit you?'

'Sad.'

'Why did you take your clothes off in nursery, dear?'

'I don't know, Mummy.'

'Okay, and do you sometimes follow Sophie about?'

'Yeah.'

'Why?'

'I don't know, Mummy.'

'You know, people don't like being followed about. It makes them feel silly. Well, thank you for telling me all this stuff, darling. Are you going to do any more hitting?'

'No.'

'Or taking your clothes off?'

'No.'

'Or following Sophie about?'

'No, Mummy.'

'Alright. Night night, pet.'

'Night night, Mummy.'

I wasn't going to quiz her anymore. It was obvious she didn't know why she did what she did, and I wasn't going to push the matter. Well, that's the official reason why I didn't pursue the matter. The real reason, however, was simply because I had no clue where or how to start tackling these issues. Was it just my parenting style? Was I inconsistent? Was I too lenient? Too strict? Did her life lack routine? Variety?

I needed to sort my head out. I needed to think. Before I had Rosemary, I would have gone for a run, 'so my brain could do its filing', as I used to say. Since becoming injured a few years back, organising and cleaning out cupboards was my new jogging. Well, it was either that or drowning my sorrows in a tub of Ben & Jerry's. I set to work on the kitchen cupboards, dragging everything out, washing down the shelves in hot soapy water. I worked like a woman possessed. My life might feel like it was spinning out of control, but at least my cupboards were clean. As I worked, I knew that I had reached my limit. I was a stressed-out bag of cats, barely holding down a job. What was I going to do if I got hauled into the CEO's office again and fired? Stay at home and live on benefits? Or soldier on with my daughter in full-time daycare when it was becoming abundantly clear that she was out of her depth in a nursery setting and just needed her mummy? My mother stayed at home and raised me and my siblings. Surely my daughter needed that, too, but then who was going to bring home the bacon? Just me. Nobody else.

I felt totally alone and overwhelmed. Tears coursed down my cheeks as I scrubbed. *You are not coping with this situation well, my girl.*

A tiny voice piped up behind me.

'Mummy?'

She made me jump.

'Oh, sorry, honey, I scratched myself by accident, and it hurts a bit, silly me.', I managed to blurt out, frantically wiping tears off my cheeks.

'I know why I do following Sophie.'

'Do you, honey?'

I peeled the rubber gloves off and turned to face my beautiful daughter.

'Yeah. She's nice.'

'Come here and give your mummy a big kiss.' I cradled her in my arms, breathing in her smell. I held her close as I rocked her gently back and forth and stroked her curls. I didn't want to be anywhere else but right there, sitting on the kitchen floor, cuddling my lovely girl. I was going to do whatever it took to help her through whatever it was she was struggling with.

By the time I woke up the next morning, I had decided what to do. I was going to seek professional help. I was going to get an appointment with a suitably qualified professional who was going to get to the bottom of all this stuff with Rosemary. All I had to do in the meantime was keep the nursery at arm's length until I had a solid plan for her future. Then, I could have a good long discussion with the manager, Sharon, about the way forward. If I could just avoid her reprimands for a little while, it would give me a little breathing space. But the admonishments were not lessening at all. By now, this was a daily occurrence. For some other people, however, my stern tellings-off halfway up the stairs were a welcome form of entertainment.

I had arrived to collect Rosemary from the nursery only to be called aside, *again*, by Sharon. While being told how naughty Rosemary had been that day, I realised that standing alongside Sharon was her young daughter, who also attended the nursery. She was clearly enjoying being privy to an adult conversation, watching, and listening.

'Rosemary's behaviour is not acceptable, and I have concerns about her development. Have you considered having her evaluated? I can refer her to the Autism Assessment Clinic from here if you like.'

The what-clinic? Did she just say the A-word?

Now I am sure this was a difficult subject for the nursery manager to broach with me. Still, I was even more uncomfortable because the manager's young daughter found this conversation so incredibly entertaining. Word must have gotten around because a few days later, when I was called aside by manager Sharon *again,* I found there to be a captive audience of about six giggling children, who were very obviously enjoying their evening entertainment, observing me receiving yet another telling off.

'Rosemary has become rather belligerent with staff, and this is becoming the rule as opposed to the exception. It has also come to my attention that some habits are . . . well . . .

less than appropriate. Only this morning, she touched her . . . her . . . private parts while she was watching TV.'

Giggle. Snigger.

'And this is not a habit we encourage young ladies to indulge in.'

Titter. Snort. Chuckle.

Right! Enough was enough.

Sharon, my dear, I am sure you are coming from a good place, but right now, you're just getting on my tits.

'Thank you, Sharon, I appreciate your feedback, however, I must point out to you that her difficult behaviour only presents itself when she is in your care. This behaviour does not happen when she's at home with me, with her grandparents, with her aunts and uncles, at church, in the park, at the beach . . .'

Exaggerate? Moi?

'. . . which begs the question, just what is going on at nursery to evoke such a response from an otherwise happy and content little girl?'

Sharon's mouth dropped open.

Aha! She wasn't expecting that, was she?

'And FYI, all kids touch their private parts from time to time, and anyone who says they don't is a liar and a prude!'

Sharon's over-plucked eyebrows had by now disappeared into her hairline.

'And another thing, I would appreciate if my confidentially and my daughter's confidentiality was respected. I am not here to provide a little light entertainment to a group of bored children.'

'Entertainment? What?'

'Bogeys at six o'clock', I quipped as I twirled a finger, motioning her to turn around.

She whirled around, spotted the young audience, and gasped. *'Upstairs! Now! All of you!'*

41

That was my cue to grab my kid and get the hell outta Dodge.

Despite our conversations, the nursery had actually been very kind to Rosemary. In fact, they had gone out of their way and had done over and above what was required of them at times. However, it was becoming evident that Rosemary was not happy at the nursery and that the nursery management was not happy with her.

The manager knew it, and I knew it—Rosemary was different.

The old childminder's poorly timed rebuke in the street rung in my ears.

Autism? Rosemary? Surely not! I got a pen and pad and sat down. This is what I wrote:

1. *Flaps her hands in front of her face.*
2. *Hops on one leg and tenses her muscles when she's excited.*
3. *Walks on her tiptoes.*
4. *The narrow range of interests and conversation topics.*
5. *The repertoire of fixed questions and answers.*
6. *Watches the same DVDs over and over.*
7. *Insists on wearing the same clothes all the time.*
8. *Speech and interaction immature compared to peers.*
9. *Prone to tantrums and aggressive outbursts, especially when in large groups of people, or noisy places.*
10. *Potty training was going well, then went backward.*
11. *Under reports pain.*
12. *Laughs hysterically for no reason, especially in bed at night.*
13. *Plays with objects that aren't toys, like flipping the light switch on and off or flushing the toilet repeatedly.*
14. *Poor eye contact.*
15. *Never gets invited to birthday parties.*

I picked up the phone.

'Okay, Sharon, you can fill out the referral form for the Autism Assessment Clinic and see if you can fast-track it as you said', I said with reluctance. 'Thank you.'

I put the phone down. Well, at least I would know for sure.

CHAPTER 4

But She's Nothing Like Rain Man

I don't know about other parts of the world, but in North West England, an autism assessment requires several appointments over several months. Rosemary was assessed by various paediatricians, speech and language therapists, occupational therapists, clinical psychologists, and the like.

Looking back, I'm sure the staff at the assessment centre must have dreaded the days my daughter and I attended because I was so oppositional with them. I just didn't want to be there, and I resented the way it was almost presumed my daughter was autistic before they'd completed all their tests.

'Excuse me; I don't think this test is being fair to Rosemary. I don't think she understands the language therapist's heavy country accent.'

I went on, determined to deliver a subtle blow somewhere, anywhere.

'I mean, *I* was desperately trying to find a *bowl,* and I couldn't find it either until I realised she was referring to a *ball.*

Rosemary thoroughly enjoyed her assessment sessions, though! She loved jumping on the mats, being pushed on the swing, and the trolley, but while she was having fun, my heart was breaking. I could view her through the two-way mirror, and there was an audio feed. I sat alone watching the assessment, watching her fail the tests, willing her to get something right.

No, Rosemary honey, put the teddy on the box, not behind it, pet.

Rosemary continued with her sessions, giggling to herself, oblivious to my heartache.

Maybe they were right about *something* being different about Rosemary. Maybe it's some gross motor skills issue, or a sensory processing disorder, or even a language delay or *something* that needs a few therapy sessions. Just not autism. Not the A-word.

'Miss Bernadette? Can you come with me please?'

Aha! This is where they are going to say that they are sorry for wasting my time, and they've discovered a little problem that can be worked on, but it's nothing to worry about.

I sat down in the consultant's office. She shuffled her paperwork and turned to me.

'We've been observing Rosemary for a few weeks now. Rosemary is a lovely little girl who likes to chat and play with the therapists, and she certainly has a good sense of fun . . .'

This was not a good start. You see, in my experience as a mother of a unique child, if it's bad news, they almost always open with a positive statement.

'But I think that you should prepare yourself that a diagnosis of autism is more probable than possible.'

My heart stopped mid-beat, then in true non-Barbie fashion, I opened my very large mouth and uttered probably the most embarrassing statement I have ever uttered in my life—and I've uttered quite a few in my time.

'But she's nothing like Rain Man!'

Yes, I said it. To all the autism parents out there, I am sorry. I am truly, truly sorry.

It is okay; you can stop cringing now.

Are you finished? Ready to get on with the story? Okay good . . . and I'm really, really, really, sorry.

I don't know how I managed to hold it together, greeting Rosemary with a smile, a hug, and still being a jolly mummy for her. I don't actually remember much about what happened later that day, but the one thing I do recall is taking Rosemary into my bed with me that night and holding her close. I lay awake, looking at my beautiful little girl while she slept so peacefully beside me. I nuzzled into her hair and breathed in the coconut scent.

I was going to have to face facts, the staff was determined to label my daughter as autistic, and I was going to have to ride this one out. Maybe I would get a second opinion and get it all sorted out later. I kissed her on the cheek, then turned around and tried to get some sleep.

It wasn't until that weekend that all the jigsaw pieces clicked into place for me. You see, up until then, Rosemary only checked a few of the autism symptoms boxes, but none of the big questions. I mean, she never lined toys up, never spun objects, she looked at people if she was comfortable in their company, and only sometimes avoided eye contact. She could talk, and she had an impish little personality.

When I took her swimming that Saturday, Rosemary spotted a little girl swimming nearby, and it was clear that Rosemary was interested in forming some sort of friendship with her. However, it was also clear that the little girl in question did not share Rosemary's sentiment. Now, most kids would make a couple of attempts at friendship and then give up but not Rosemary. She followed the girl about the swimming pool, oblivious to the obvious cues that she did not want to play. This went on for a while, and the other girl became more and more distressed as Rosemary relentlessly followed her about the pool.

'Rosemary, honey, I don't think she wants to be friends. Never mind. Just enjoy yourself and have a swim about until the session is over.'

'Okay, mummy.'

She promptly resumed her pursuit of the little girl.

By this time, the girl had burst into tears and ran into her mother's arms. Rosemary duly followed her and stood there, much too close, smiling at her. The child's sobs turned into full-blown wails.

Oops! This is not good!

'Attention all bathers', came the loudspeaker announcement. 'The morning bathing session has now finished. Please vacate the pool at your earliest convenience.'

Thank God for that.

'Okay, kiddo, time to go!'

'Sorry about that. If she follows a kid around like that, it means she likes her . . .' I trailed off. Othermum nodded.

I didn't say much as I got my daughter changed. She happily chatted with me about the new friend she made while I made lots of noises to show interest, but my mind was elsewhere. How could she not see that the girl did not want to be friends?

I brought her home and went about preparing lunch.

'How about some colouring-in for a change? There you go. Here are some papers and pens, and I'll just be in the kitchen, pet.'

Now that's good, colouring-in instead of Barbies! I spied Barbie on the kitchen counter and gave her the finger. *Hah! Not so popular now, are you Barbie dearest?* I made a quick sandwich and salad for us both—time to eat.

'Okay, Rosemary, time for . . . *Oh, my God!*'

There it was, a perfectly straight line of pens. End to end. From one corner of the room to the other.

My daughter was lining things up.

My daughter was autistic.

CHAPTER 5

The Day a Part of Me Died

'The team is ready for you now, Miss Bernadette', the receptionist smiled.

I walked into the room. Behind the desk were all the practitioners who had been assessing Rosemary at the clinic over the past few months, but today I didn't have my little companion with me. Rosemary was at the nursery.

'Miss Bernadette. Thank you for coming. I think you've probably met most people here, but could we just start by introducing everyone?'

I smiled and nodded as each clinician was introduced.

'Okay, so we've all observed Rosemary at various times over the past few weeks, and we've also had a brief consultation already. Rosemary certainly is a lovely child, and she really is a credit to you. However, upon reflection, we are of the unanimous opinion that . . .'

'That Rosemary is autistic', I concluded for her.

Pause.

'Yes.'

'Yes, I think so, too.'

Surprised glances were exchanged behind the desk.

'Erm . . . there are a couple of seminars you can attend. Rosemary will also require some speech and language, as well as occupational therapy sessions.'

'To help her?', I ventured.

'Help her?' The paediatrician looked puzzled. 'Well, yes, in a way', she continued. 'The seminars would be more for your benefit so you can understand her condition a bit better. And some speech and OT will help Rosemary a bit, but . . .'

She cleared her throat before she continued.

'Perhaps when you've had a chance to digest the news, you might want to consider a social worker for her. You should also visit special schools in the area as quickly as you can. If she's already struggling at nursery, she would definitely need the additional supports a special school could provide.'

'But, she's obviously high functioning.', one of the therapists volunteered.

I had no clue what high functioning meant, but one thing I did know was my daughter had the A-word. My daughter had autism.

'Yes, she's high functioning. Therefore, she may well be able to cope in adulthood if she were to secure a place in a supported living environment, which, of course, would be preferable to placing her in full-time care.'

My heart stopped.

Did she just say full-time care? Like an institution?

'With a bit of help, she might even be able to hold down a little part-time job, you know. Employers are very inclusive these days—supermarkets, garden centres, and such. But that's a long way off. Best to focus on the now.'

'Supported living? You mean like a special needs home?'

'Yes, that would be the preferred outcome.'

'As opposed to an institution?'

Awkward pause.

'Yes.'

'Are you saying that she will end up in one of these places?'

Another awkward pause.

'It is possible.', came the reply.

I swallowed hard.

'Autism is a lifelong condition, Miss Bernadette. You can't change it.'

She cleared her throat again. 'So, if I could have all the professionals' signatures, we can give the diagnosis to Miss Bernadette.'

With the last signature, the piece of paper was handed over the desk. I looked at it—one A4 page with scrawled handwriting.

Following assessment, Rosemary Bernadette has been diagnosed with Autistic Spectrum Disorder.

My daughter had been summed up in one abrupt sentence.

'I love her, and I'm proud of her', I said. Then, I left.

A part of me died that day. My daughter had autism. I did not have the little girl I thought I had. The one I hoped would go to university, travel the world, have a job she loved, and maybe have children of her own. The Rosemary I had would never do any of these things. She had autism, a lifelong condition, and she was going to have to live in a special needs home when she got older, if she was lucky.

I started up the car engine, but what was playing on the radio just couldn't do it for me. A few bars of the pina colada song wasn't going to cut it that day, so I popped in one of Rosemary's CD audiobooks instead. I parked the car at my house and sat there, engine running. The facts sunk in deeper. Rosemary had autism. She might be able to hold down a job if she had a lot of support and would probably have to live in supported accommodation when I become too old to care for her. Her life would be run by a bunch of social workers doing a perfunctory job of managing her. What sort of life would that be for her? Where would she get the love that she so craved? Who would provide that? Her future looked bleak. The enormity of the situation reared up like a huge black cloud in front of me. The unfairness of it. The hopelessness of it. I felt sick to my stomach.

God, whatever I've done, whoever I've hurt, I never deserved this.

I sat a while longer. The future was a dark and frightening place, way too much for me to handle. I had to focus on the now, just like the consultant said. I needed to educate myself on autism and also find the right school for her, a place where they would understand her. She needed speech and language, and occupational therapy, and I was going to ensure she got whatever she needed.

Just take baby steps, Ruthangela. Just a little at a time.

I turned the ignition and audiobook off. Slowly, I turned the key in the lock and let myself into my house. It was cold and uninviting. I sat at the kitchen table, blinds drawn, and my head in my hands. The silence was deafening. I must have sat like that for over an hour, unflinching.

So this is what it feels like when your heart breaks in two.

Later that night, I rang my parents.

'Well now she's even more special', said my mum.

'You give her a big kiss from us and tell her we love her', said my dad.

'And I wouldn't change a hair on her head', added Mum. 'She's perfect the way she is.'

'And we love you, too!', interjected Dad.

I had good family support. I was going to need it. If she attended a special school with their expertise in special children, I might be able to lean on them, too.

CHAPTER 6

Dying Just a Little Bit More

The educational psychologist sat across the kitchen table from me. She looked young.

Cow.

'I think Rosemary would be much happier in a school environment specifically designed for children on the spectrum', she said with a flick of her Barbie-like hair.

'Okay.'

Where are my scissors?

'I understand she never really settled at the nursery?'

'No, not really. She would run around a lot and even tried to escape a few times. I think the staff called her The Runner. It was a kind of pet name they had for her . . .' I trailed off, blushing at what I had just said.

'Hmmm, The Runner. I see.'

The educational psychologist began to prattle on about an assessment for a Statement of Educational Needs. But to be honest, all I could hear was Beyoncé singing "Runnin"[6].

'And when the statement's ready, I have a particular school in mind for her. They are very experienced in dealing with autism, you know. The class sizes are much smaller, about five or six children in each class, with one teacher and three teaching assistants.'

'Wow, now that's Rosemary's kind of class.'

'All the staff is used to teaching children with social communication difficulties; so she will be in good hands there. She can get the school bus every day, and her educational provision will be as per what is set out in the Statement of Educational Needs. Miss Bernadette . . . Miss Bernadette?'

"Runnin', runnin', runnin' ain't runnin' from myself no more."

'Miss Bernadette?'

'Sorry! I was miles away! Please go on. Yes, erm . . . statement, yes.'

I jerked myself out of my daydream and sat back up straight. 'Tell me, even though it's a special school, she'll still be taught all the normal mainstream stuff? You know, reading, writing, maths, and the like? Rosemary is a bright child, you know. I don't want her missing out on anything.'

'Oh, the school will see to her academic work as well, that won't be a problem, not at all. No, they will be following the curriculum, just like any other school.', she assured me.

I thanked the girl for her time, saying I would sleep on it and get back to her. Choosing the right school for my kid, now with a diagnosis of autism, was not a decision I was going to take lightly.

I closed the door behind her and went back into the kitchen, my mind focussed at last. Five or six kids in the class and four staff members? Also, the staff was used to looking after autistic children, according to the educational psychologist. I knew very little about the subject myself, being so new to this whole autism thing. These teachers would certainly be a valuable resource for me, a much-needed font of information. Also, the teacher-pupil ratio was pretty impressive, especially since Rosemary struggled in large groups. Even if I had the money to pay for private education, the teacher to pupil ratio would still be nowhere near as good.

A few days later, Rosemary and I had an appointment to look around the special school. I wanted both of us to feel calm for the visit, so I played Rosemary's audiobook again as we drove the forty-minute journey. It was "Mr Stink" by David Walliams[7], which was one of my ingenious ideas to help Rosemary with her receptive language difficulties. We let his dulcet tones fill the car as we negotiated the winding country lanes.

"Mr Stink stank. He also stunk. And if it was correct English to say he stinked, then he stinked as well. He was the stinkiest stinker that ever lived . . ."

Rosemary giggled the whole way there.

It was an old school building. The receptionist asked us to wait, and we did. The corridor was so silent that I could easily have heard a pin drop, suddenly making me feel uneasy. I held little Rosemary's hand tight as she scanned the strange new surroundings, eyes like huge blue saucers.

My stomach lurched. I'd been feeling decidedly unwell all morning; it must have been nerves.

'Hi, Rosemary!'

We looked up, and around the corner tottered the tiniest adult woman I have ever set eyes on. She held out her hand to Rosemary, who gave hers in return.

'Are you coming to have a look around the school today?'

Rosemary nodded.

Off they went, hand in hand. From behind, they looked like two little schoolgirls skipping along the corridor together.

'You can come, too, mummy!' she shouted over her shoulder.

Well, Rosemary seems to like the teacher alright, I thought to myself.

The obligatory school tour then ensued. I nodded and smiled politely, and Rosemary seemed happy enough. She was particularly pleased to see the soft play area.

'We bring a child here from time to time to help them calm down when they are feeling overwhelmed, and they just bounce their troubles away!', explained the teacher with a wave.

Whoa!

Despite Mrs Giles's diminutive stature, her pits packed a mean punch. I put my hand to my mouth.

'A school with a soft play area?' *Cough! Cough!* 'This is novel!'

'Yes, we certainly find it useful. And you can see the playground over there.'

She lifted her arm and pointed, freeing up another moist armpit.

Waft!

I felt decidedly nauseous.

'Oh, yes, can I have a look?'

I need some fresh air here. I headed for the door.

'What? Going out into the rain? You're brave!'

No, just keeping breakfast down, love.

'Actually, we can cut through the playground on the way back from the assembly hall if you like, if you just come with me, I can show you.'

On they went. I let her and Rosemary go first. *Stay upwind of her Ruthangela.* Rosemary was either oblivious to her body odour, or she was handling the unfortunate olfactory situation incredibly well.

We all padded down the hall. My brain hit the play button on the audiobook.

"Mr Stink stank. He also stunk. And if it was correct English to say he stinked, then he stinked as well. He was the stinkiest stinker that ever lived . . ."

Be quiet!

"A stink is the worst type of smell. A stink is worse than a stench. And a stench is worse than a pong . . ."

Think of something else quick!

'Erm, what sports do the children play?'

'Oh, glad you asked, we're in the process of building a soccer and netball pitch. You can see where the workmen have been digging there.'

'Oh, yes, behind the stench. I mean fence!'

She gave me a quizzical look, and my cheeks turned pink.

Fence, you idiot! Fence!

'I said fence!' My cheeks reddened.

"And a pong is worse than a whiff. And a whiff can be enough to make your nose wrinkle . . ."

Shut up!

'Erm . . . erm . . . and where would the classroom be then?'

'Just up these stairs here', she said with a flourish.

Waft!

Cough! Cough!

'Are you alright Mizzsssscccch Bernadette?'

Are you kidding me?

'Just a tickle, I'm fine. Please lead the way.'

Despite her odour, I found the teacher to be a pleasant enough woman. After an hour or so, either I had become accustomed to the smell, or I had learned the art of breathing through my mouth. I started to relax.

'So, what are the teaching methods then?', I asked.

There was a pause.

'How do you mean?'

'Well, isn't it specialised teaching for children on the spectrum?'

There was another pause.

'Does the teaching method have a name? Something I could research for myself?'

'We do a bit of TEACCH.'

TEACCH[8]. I had read something about that. I racked my brains, then I remembered it was about adapting the environment to make it more autism-friendly and that parents worked collaboratively on a co-therapist basis with teachers. More importantly, there was an understanding that any difficult behaviour was due to underlying problems in perception and understanding, rather than just being naughty.

'I've read a bit about TEACCH, but I could do with a little more education.', I explained.

'Well, there are some books around the place. I'm sure we could lend you a few if you wanted.', offered Mrs Giles.

This was probably the right place for Rosemary, I thought to myself. The school certainly appeared to check all the boxes:

Classes designed for children with social communication difficulties ✔
Specialist teaching staff and classroom assistants ✔
Small class sizes ✔
Great teacher-pupil ratio ✔
Soft play area ✔
Learning for me ✔
Teacher hygiene . . . let's leave that for another day

On paper, this was definitely the right school for us. I signed the admission documents. I sat back in the chair and sipped my tea as Rosemary played in the corner.

I should be excited about this, I thought to myself. *So why do I feel so deflated?* I had an uneasy feeling in my stomach, and it wasn't nausea from earlier. No, something just wasn't right.

Mrs Giles seemed a nice lady, and Rosemary seemed to take to her alright. But I wasn't completely sold, not for any particular reason. Okay, so she had a little personal hygiene thing going on. Maybe she was allergic to something in the deodorant. But the uneasy feeling in my gut told me that something was amiss. I couldn't quite put my finger on it, just that it all felt so very wrong.

Have you ever been in a position where someone isn't quite sure if you are a Miss or a Mrs? So, rather than just ask you or look at the application form in front of their noses, they end up calling you Mizzsssscccch instead. Not Ms—Mizzsssscccch, a combination of the sounds of Miss, Mrs, and Ms.

'Rosemary is a clever little girl, Mrs Giles. I am very keen for her to be given the same opportunities as other children.'

'Yes, of course, Mizzsssscccch Bernadette.'

'Promise me one thing. Promise me her academics will receive equal attention.'

'I promise, Mizzsssscccch Bernadette.'

I exhaled.

'Great, thank you. So, we'll see you in a few weeks then?'

I held my breath as we shook hands. It was done; my daughter was going to be attending a special school. My heart sank.

You're doing the right thing, Ruthangela, I comforted myself on the way home. No matter how many times I said it, and no matter how many times I examined the facts objectively, something didn't feel good.

I switched on the car stereo.

"It wasn't Mr Stink's fault that he stank . . ." David Walliams' voice filled the car.

'Mr Stink!', exclaimed Rosemary.

'Yes, dear. Do you think Mr Stink would like to go to your new school, too?'

My little companion giggled.

I drove the forty-minute journey back home, with my heart trailing behind.

PART II

The Steps

CHAPTER 7

Autism Treatment Centre

The months passed, I had accepted Rosemary's autism diagnosis, and gotten on with our lives. Rosemary had completed her first year at her special school and travelled there each day on the bus. She seemed happy enough.

'Guess what, Mummy? My teacher did got me Barbies to play with!'

'Did she, pet? That was nice.'

'I do play with them when I be good.'

It was rare that Rosemary told me much about her school day. I usually had to pull the information out of her like extracting a wisdom tooth, but of course, Barbie news was big news and required no extraction whatsoever. In fact, I rarely received any useful feedback from the school at all, so what went on behind the school gates was, more often than not, a mystery.

I started to educate myself about my daughter's condition. I attended the NHS seminars the paediatrician recommended, but I found them totally inappropriate for Rosemary's needs. I learned very quickly that autism for one child was entirely different from another. There's a saying in the autism community: 'If you've met one child with autism, you've met one child with autism.', and it's very apt.[9] I turned to books on the subject, joined a couple of autism organisations, anything to gain more knowledge on the subject.

My back was hurting. One morning, when the pain had become unbearable, I managed to see Rosemary off on the school bus, then dialled 999. I was unwell, very unwell.

A trip to A&E, more painkillers than I care to remember, and an MRI scan later, my condition was diagnosed. I had a slipped disc, and I was in constant agony. I was going to have to take a few months off work and recuperate.

Rosemary heard me struggling to get changed in the bedroom.

'Are you okay, Mummy?'

'Yes, darling, just having a hard time getting changed', I said through clenched teeth.

'Is your back sick, Mummy?'

'Yes, sweetheart. I have a sick back.'

'I helping you. Lie down, Mummy.'

Then my baby girl undressed me and put my pyjamas on for me, just like that. No drama, no bother.

'Rosemary! What a clever girl you are! Thank you so much! That was so helpful!'

'Okay, mummy.'

That kid's going to be a nurse when she grows up! I thought to myself for a moment, just a brief little moment, then reality hit. Rosemary was *not* going to be a nurse actually because Rosemary was autistic. Rosemary had the A-word.

You need to stop thinking like that Ruthangela. This is the new Rosemary, not the Rosemary you thought you had.

I sighed and pulled my slippers on. Now that I was going to be off work for several months, I could use the time to educate myself further on the subject of autism. I read and googled as much as I dared. And because I was unable to sit still for prolonged periods, I found myself sprawled out on the sofa in front of the television when the pain got too much.

Looking back on this period of my life, I realise time has very generously afforded me a little wisdom. Yes, it was an awful time, and I felt absolutely wretched, but it was also the luckiest few months of my life. Had I not been lying on the sofa watching not-so-riveting daytime television one particular morning, that fleeting thought might never have fluttered into my under-utilised brain. This notion entered my thoughts during a talk show, just as I was working up the energy to get up off the sofa and make myself a cuppa.

With more and more kids being diagnosed autistic, and so many of them needing extra support with language, occupational therapy, and digestive issues, I'm sure there must be an autism centre somewhere that offers all the therapies and treatments in one place, like a one-stop-shop . . .

I was so bored that day, I acted upon this transient idea right there and then. Well, let's face it; I had nothing better to do.

If you are a daytime chat show host and you are reading this book, I am sure your shows are both relevant and informative. I fully accept that some of your guests may own a full set of teeth, but your television shows aren't my cup of tea. Sorry.

I got up and hobbled over to the computer and typed into Google three words:

"Autism Treatment Centre".

The search result in front of my eyes that day completely changed the course of our lives.

69

The Autism Treatment Center of America[10]. I clicked on the link and started to read all about their Son-Rise Program.

"Your child's potential is limitless", the website said. "While we certainly cannot predict what any given child will achieve, we do not believe any child or parent is served when others decide in advance what that child will not achieve". I stopped dead in my tracks. The paediatrician had decided in advance what my daughter could and could not achieve in her lifetime. She told me that she might have to be institutionalised, or live in a group home if she was lucky. She had given up on my child and had written off her entire life in a heartbeat, yet here was an organisation in America completely at odds with the paediatrician. "You won't give up on your child. Neither will we." Did I read that right? My hands froze on the keyboard as I felt my heart skip a beat.

Oh, my god, Ruthangela, have you given up on Rosemary?

Had I given up on her? Had I sent her off to a special school on the bus each day, rather like the mother who just closes the door to the messy room because she knows if she looks inside, she won't like what she sees? Had I packed her off for the day thinking what the eyes don't see, the heart doesn't grieve over?

Was I going to write my daughter off just like the paediatrician had, and resign myself to the fact that she was destined for some sort of special living arrangement by the time she reached adulthood? Or was I going to believe in my daughter? Would I . . . *dare* I believe that my daughter could achieve much more than what the paediatrician predicted for her?

I watched some of the before and after videos and read the testimonials from parents about how much progress their child had made, how some previously nonverbal children were suddenly speaking in sentences. I watched another video of a young man graduating from university as his parents proudly recalled the day they first heard of The Son-Rise Program. The sceptic in me said, '*Hmmm, if it appears too good to be true, it probably is*', but my heart told me to read on, and I did. In fact, I lost all track of the time that day. Back pain? What back pain? Before I knew it, my daughter had arrived home. Much as I loved the little mite, I couldn't wait until she went off to school the next day so I could get online again.

The following day, I sat down in front of the computer and went straight to The Son-Rise Program website. I sifted through more information, and my brain absorbed every last drop of it.

In less than a week, I received their DVDs in the post, and one of their advisors, Brian, had called me. Several phone calls and emails passed between us. I picked every single bit of information out of that poor man's head. He was a father to a child who had completed The Son-Rise Program and was doing well in school. I was fascinated.

For any of you who are not familiar with The Son-Rise Program, let me give you the low-down.

The Son-Rise Program is a behavioural therapy programme that is led and run by a parent. It is based upon accepting your child as they are, rather than forcing a child to conform. The parent joins with the child in their repetitive behaviours. The child's "stims", or "isms" are copied or "joined" and used as motivation to learn new skills. I decided to run a trial with a few Son-Rise sessions at home with Rosemary to see what would happen since my back was getting stronger now, and I felt up to the challenge.

'Now remember, if you are playing with Rosemary, and she stops and flaps her hands in front of her face, you should flap your hands, too, okay?' Brian said.

'Got it!'

'Just focus on joining with Rosemary for the first few sessions, okay?'

'Got it!'

'And remember the three E's.'

'Energy, excitement, and enthusiasm!'

Brian laughed. 'You're good to go! I'll call you to see how you get on. When's a good day?'

So, without any formal training, I made my first tentative steps into Rosemary's Son-Rise Program.

The programme called for a dedicated playroom, free from any distraction, but my living room would have to do for the time being.

The next day was a Saturday—our first Son-Rise day!

'When does my special playtime be starting mummy?' Rosemary asked over the breakfast table.

'Soon, pet, when you've digested your breakfast properly.'

Every few minutes, Rosemary would enquire about when her playtime would start. She was so excited!

The Son-Rise Program depends upon the child showing us the way into their world, then when the time is right, the parent shows the child the way out. Into Rosemary's world, I went head first! Our play consisted of . . . take a wild guess . . . yep, you guessed it . . . Barbies! I joined with lots of enthusiasm as you're supposed to. I found myself enjoying changing their clothes and going to the shops, on holidays, to the park, wherever Rosemary dictated. She could be a right little bossy boots. Out of the corner of my eye, I could see Rosemary begin to flap her hands, so I flapped, too, with all seriousness, then resumed play. This joining of mine certainly did not go un-noticed. A few minutes later, she tensed up the muscles in her arms and face, a movement she tended to do when she was excited. I joined in and tensed up, too. I could see the amusement in Rosemary's face. Have you ever been able to *see* your child thinking? It's almost as if you can see the cogs physically moving within your child's mind. I watched Rosemary watching me, and I swear I saw her internal cogs move as she thought about hatching her delicious plan. Next, Rosemary stood up, held her arms aloft, and shouted, 'Ah! Ah! Ah!', which was something she had never done before. I joined in this "stim", to Rosemary's roars of laughter. She did it again, and I obliged, again. Rosemary was bent over double, laughing hysterically. Miss Madam was inventing "stims" just to watch me copy her, which of course, was a source of immense amusement to her.

Our first Son-Rise session lasted three hours, and we had a blast. Brian found Miss Madam's antics hilarious. He was thrilled: 'She was obviously very aware of you joining with her. She must have been observing a lot. This is a great start!' He urged.

More Son-Rise sessions followed. There was plenty of information on their website to keep me going. As the weeks turned into months, I had to think seriously about embarking upon a proper at-home programme for her. Was it just good fun playing with her, or was this programme going to reduce her autistic behaviours in the long run? I knew that a Son-Rise Program could last anything from six months to six years, so was I in or was I out? I was faced with a choice—do the sensible thing and support Rosemary as best I could with her lifelong condition, or I could learn The Son-Rise Program technique instead. Whatever decision I took, I knew I was going to have to live with it. Another issue was the cost. The Start-Up Program was expensive, plus return flights to America.

'But what if this crowd takes your money, drags you to the States and back, all for a load of old rubbish? You'll never see that money again!', reasoned my father, and he had a point; it was possible.

'But this won't change Rosemary's personality, will it?' My mum was concerned. 'I would hate it if this thing changed her. I love her sunny little ways.'

'Actually, I don't think it will. What I've researched says that some other therapies in the past made some kids come across as a bit robotic, but Son-Rise isn't supposed to be like that.'

'I don't know, Ruthangela. It all seems a bit whacko. How can copying a child help them? I'm worried you'll get scammed.'

'I know, I know, Dad. I'm worried about it, too, but I would rather do it and get conned out of a couple of thousand dollars than never do it at all. I'm the one that will have to live with myself having never bothered even to try, and I don't think I can do that.'

'I see nothing wrong with her, nothing at all. She's just Rosemary to me.'

'But she has autism, Mum.'

'Why must they put a label on absolutely everything these days?'

That night I woke up with a start, sat up in bed and turned on the light. I ruminated over my conversation with my parents earlier. At worst, I would lose some money, but it's only money. Rosemary would be no better and no worse off, and she will have had a great time during our Son-Rise play sessions to boot. That was the worst-case scenario. My mind was made up. If I tried and failed, then at least I had tried. I could live with myself then. There would be no what-ifs. This was something I simply had to do.

It was summertime, and Rosemary still attended the nursery during school holiday periods. Since my parents would be looking after Rosemary in their own home and she would not be attending nursery, I rang Sharon to explain her absence for a week.

'Oh, the Son-Rise thingy? Yes, someone was telling me about that the other day that some family from around here went to that. So, you're off to America to learn all that stuff then? Okay. Just . . . just . . . don't . . .', she trailed off.

'Just don't . . .?', I probed.

'Just don't get your hopes up.'

I reserved my spot on the course and booked my flight. I was in.

Daytime television is awesome.

CHAPTER 8

Son-Rise

I stared out of the plane window. I was on my way to The Son-Rise Program Start-Up! I had forgotten how easy air travel was when you didn't have an autistic six-year-old with you. It was hard leaving my daughter behind, but she was with my parents, so she was in safe hands.

'Promise me you won't change her personality', my mum's pleadings resounded in my head. Well, that certainly wasn't going to happen, not if I could help it. I sat back and closed my eyes, smiling to myself as I imagined what she might be doing right now—waking up, jumping into her grandparents' bed for a cuddle, having breakfast, going to the park. My whole life revolved around my daughter. I knew it wasn't healthy for me, never taking any me-time, but if I was going to embark upon a Son-Rise Program for Rosemary, I was going to have to dedicate serious hours to it. My needs would have to take a back seat for another few years yet, and I was okay with that. Rosemary came first and always would.

Apart from a three-hour delay, the flight was pretty uneventful. Next, I had to catch the shuttle bus to Grand Central Station, then a train off to the Berkshires, where I caught a taxi from the train station. By the time I got there, it was long after dark. As the car turned into the grounds of the Option Institute, its headlights illuminated a sign on the wall.

'A place for miracles.'

Bloody hell, I grimaced.

I've been swindled.

I felt sick to my stomach.

Miracles? What sort of hippie set-up is this? They'll have us hugging trees next!

Annoyances aside, I was weary from the day's travel, and I wanted nothing else but sleep. I was directed to my lodgings for the week and fell into bed, fully clothed, and falling asleep before my head hit the pillow.

If I had done my research properly, I would have realised that the reference to miracles was probably a nod to Barry Neil (Bears) Kaufman's books, "A Miracle to Believe in"[11] and "Son Rise—The Miracle Continues"[12], which I didn't read until a couple of years after.

The next morning I was up early, showering, unpacking, and getting to know my roommate, Zoe, from New York State. She had driven there and arrived even later than I had. I was so soundly asleep when she arrived that I didn't stir as she let herself into the room, unpacked, showered, and got into her bed.

Zoe and I sat down to breakfast.

'What did you think of the sign on the wall on your way in?'

'Sign? I didn't see a sign.'

'It said, "A Place for Miracles."'

Zoe smiled. Then, she saw my raised eyebrow, and her smile broadened.

'That's American-ese for you!', she whispered.

'In America, everything is awesome, and people are always super-excited! Nothing's ever just nice or fine, you know.'

It was my turn to smile. I was glad I had asked.

'So, you don't think it's all a bit new-age then?'

'Nah, not really. I mean it's not as if they are serving tofu for breakfast, is it?'

She was right; it all seemed pretty normal so far. There wasn't a gypsy skirt or a dream catcher in sight. People were attending the same programme from all walks of life, and I began to relax. Everyone was friendly, and not in drum-beating kind of way either.

Overreact? Moi?

We chatted some more, and I found out that she was married with three kids, all of whom were on the spectrum. She told me that she was really here for her middle child, Lilly, who was more severely affected than her two higher functioning siblings. Zoe was a full-time mum who home-schooled.

Home-school mum? This girl deserves a medal. I would never be able to do that!

We found our way to the lecture room and sat down. We each received a huge ring binder crammed full of programme materials. I practically salivated, but as soon as I opened it and studied the Option Institute map, I frowned.

'Hey, Zoe, I thought we were in Massachusetts, but this map says Connecticut.'

'Yeah, it's both. The state line cuts through the campus, so half of it is in Connecticut and the other half in Massachusetts. Our room and this lecture room are in Connecticut, but if you go past the lake, you'd be in Massachusetts.'

'But they're both in the same time zone, right?'

'Right.'

'Pity, could have gotten an hour's extra sleep in there somewhere.'

The course started. I had watched a lot of videos online and recognised the tutors immediately. I found myself feeling a bit coy, or was I starstruck?

Wow, these tutors got us. I mean they *really* got us. It was so refreshing having an autism professional who totally understands where autism parents are coming from. Bryn Hogan was the first tutor to introduce herself. She was one of the Kaufman's daughters, and had helped out with her brother Raun's Son-Rise Program, then later with her own daughter Jade, with her husband, William. In the middle of one of her sessions, she said, 'You are the expert on your child's autism. Nobody will ever understand your child's needs more than you. Trust your gut instinct; it's always right.' This was the first instruction of many that struck a chord with me. She was so right. I thought back to meetings with educators and clinicians back home, the manner in which they conversed with one another in almost a code-like manner, while I sat at the table feeling left out of the Clever People's Club. To be told that I was the expert on my daughter was not only refreshing but so liberating!

They handed out copies of The Son-Rise Program Developmental Model. It was a detailed document, mapping out all the specific programme goals broken down into five stages. I had a quick look at it, and my eye fell on one section in particular, "Flexibility." Rosemary could certainly be inflexible at times, especially if she was feeling uncomfortable. I remember joking with my family during a game of cards one evening. 'It's only snap when Rosemary says so!' Yes, she was definitely a controlling little lady.

I sat and pondered a minute. Somehow, I knew, I just knew that if I unlocked flexibility in my daughter, it would unlock the remainder of the programme. Finally, I was listening to my gut instinct, and it was right.

After lunch, it was William Hogan's session. He started by describing how he worked with a child with a very specific high functioning stim. He knew everything about the London underground system. He read voraciously on the subject, hoarding documents and maps. He talked incessantly about trains, stations, the different tube lines, and he got upset if he was told to stop. My ears pricked up. Now, if I just substituted the word tube or train with Barbie, we'd be on the right track, no pun intended. This was my kind of lecture!

'He was so knowledgeable! Being an Englishman myself, I'm familiar with London, so I was able to ask him how to get from A to B, and this little guy knew exactly how to negotiate his way around the tube stations, even at which platform the train stopped. He knew his stuff!' William's eyes gleamed as he told the story.

'He even had a favourite station!' He went on.

'The name of the station was . . .' William paused for a second, almost mid-air. It was as if he was having a slight memory lapse and was frantically trying to remember the name of it.

'It was called . . . F . . . F . . . Fo . . . Fo . . . erm . . . Cokmosst . . .'

Now, as I am sure you've gathered by now, I bit of language never bothered me. But, I was in America, and one thing I did know was that Americans don't like naughty words. Another thing I was sure about was that William was going to drop the F-bomb any fucking second.

I closed my eyes and prayed, not for me, but for the Americans around me.

'Don't let him say the F word, please don't let him say the F word!'

William continued to struggle, 'Fo . . . uh, Cockmosst . . .'

At this point in my mind, William had gone into slow motion.

Oh, God, he's going to say it.

'F . . . Fo . . . Fo . . .'

I couldn't stand it any longer.

'*Cockfosters!*', I shouted at the top of my voice!

'*Cockfosters*! That's it! Thank you! You've no idea what I was about to say!', William said to the group.

I exhaled with relief.

As the day wore on, the subject matter changed. It was time for questions.

'Is going GFCF recommended at the same time?' someone at the back of the room asked.

'What on earth is GFCF?', I asked the girl beside me.'

'Gluten and casein-free', she whispered. I had become friendly with a woman from Texas, Kym, who had two teenage sons, both on the spectrum, high functioning.

I must have looked puzzled.

'Casein is in dairy. Lots of kids are on the diet, even if they're not allergic. It helps a lot', she drawled.

'Gluten and dairy make their autism symptoms worse by causing inflammation in the gut that spreads to the brain. That's why some of them act stoned or hyper after eating certain foods. They have an opiate effect.'

William asked the group for a show of hands whose kid was currently eating a GFCF diet. I looked around. About eighty percent of hands were in the air.

'And if you don't think it helps much, take your hand down', William said. I watched. Not one single hand lowered—not one.

'What about school lunches when you're GFCF?' came another question.

'Lunch at school is whatever was for dinner the night before. Cook in bulk', was the concise reply.

Hmmm. Do gluten and casein affect how a child thinks and feels? How can that be? Did I really want to restrict my daughter's diet? Don't I have enough to deal with at the moment? I decided to put the idea to the back of my mind—for now.

'Use up the food in the cupboards first when you get home. But as you transition into the diet, it's probably easier if the whole family goes GFCF, because your kids are going to be like little crack addicts looking for their next wheat or dairy fix. And believe me, if you have it hidden away in the cupboard, they'll find it!'

The audience tittered.

'No, I'm serious. Some of our kids are addicted to gluten and dairy. If you're going GFCF, you have to be 100% committed. Think about it, is it a good idea to give an addict just a little bit of cocaine every now and then as a treat? No. It will be the same for you guys, but it can be worth it. GFCF works for a lot of kids, though not all. So, you need to decide if it's something you want to try or not.'

'And what about the window? What happens if you run out of time?'

'The window?', I whispered to Kym.

'Yeah, there's a window of opportunity for a good result. I think it shuts when the kid's about five.'

I felt the panic rise. Rosemary would be seven in a few months. Was I too late?

'No, we treat people in their fifties here at The Son-Rise Program. Significant progress can be made at any age', said William.

Just put that one to the back of your mind, too, there's plenty of room.

'But if your kid's looking at you, they won't look at the book.'

'The more they look, the more they learn. For now; leave the academics, it will come in time. They'll catch up', came William's reply.

I found out that many kids were home-schooled because their parents couldn't find an appropriate school for them. But to take your child out of school and educate them at home? I wasn't up to it. And even if I was, how on earth could I afford it? I *had* to work.

I managed to get William on his own for a couple of minutes to ask him about noisy, echoing environments, such as the swimming pool, kids' jungle gyms, etc. Rosemary really loved going to these sorts of places, even though she would frequently meltdown when there. William listened intently as I chattered on and on.

Talkative? Moi?

He smiled patiently. He really was a gentleman, the old-fashioned sort. The lectures were already running behind schedule, but William didn't seem to mind me commandeering him in the hallway at all.

'Just make sure she isn't "isming" on the apparatus, and when it's time to go, she has to come without a fuss. Otherwise, you might need to get in more playroom time before you go there again.'

I thanked him and looked at my watch. It was time for the High Functioning Breakout Session in another part of the campus, and I was late. I ran the whole way there, flinging open the door of the Option House with a bang. I stood there for a moment, holding on to the doorframe, panting. Everyone turned around to look at me.

Silence.

'Sorry I'm late. I ran all the way from Connecticut.'

There were only six parents at this session, and I quizzed Kate Wilde over Rosemary's repertoire of questions that required the stock answer from me.

'She will ask these questions to seek familiarity and security. She's testing your predictability. She's asking, "Is this okay? Can I trust you?"'

I was speechless. It made complete sense. Usually, she asked these questions when she was feeling uneasy in some way. If I remember correctly, these conversations almost always seemed to happen directly after any sort of hullabaloo at nursery. I cast my mind back and recalled the events. Of course! The questions came thick and fast just after she had witnessed me getting a dressing down by the nursery management! She was a sensitive soul. She felt my humiliation, my frustration. She needed to be comforted, to be reassured that everything was going to be alright. Well, the Son-Rise manual does say you need to be the happy detective. Jessica Fletcher's got nothing on me.

'You can test for green lights when you're having these conversations. Say you were to give her a silly answer instead, if she laughs, that's a green light. Or you could whisper or sing the answer, dance around, do something different, and watch her reaction. If she corrects you, that's a red light.'

My mind was racing. This was going to work! Since I arrived at the Option Institute, these tutors had been on the money in terms of understanding my child.

'If you see her body relaxing or she pauses when asking you these questions, that could be a green light, too.'

Someone understands my child! My wrist was aching by this point as I was feverishly scribbling in my notepad. This was golden!

That night, I sat up in bed, looking over my notes from the day. I was truly blessed. I had just one child on the spectrum, while some parents had two and three. My child could speak when most of the parents here for the week had never heard their child say, 'Mummy' or 'Daddy.' Some of these parents had children that never looked at them, ate only one or two specific foods, smeared their faeces on walls, or slept for only two hours each night. I, on the other hand, had a beautiful little girl who looked at me, was able to converse with me, and she had the most endearing little personality. I was blessed, truly blessed.

I sent a quick email to my parents. "How's Rosemary? Love you lots. Ruthangela x." I smiled and turned off my tablet.

I was the first person in the lecture theatre the next morning, front row.

'They show us the way into their world, and when they're ready, we show them the way out', said Bryn.

I had remembered that quote from the movie about Raun K. Kaufman and his family, "Son-Rise: A Miracle of Love"[13]. Bryn was talking again about joining with your child in their stims, or "isms," as they preferred to say. The more she explained this joining process, the more sense it made. I mean, how cool would it be to *finally* meet someone who likes the same stuff that you like? Someone who really gets you? No wonder children with poor eye contact were suddenly starting to look at the people who loved spinning plates just as much as they did!

The next session was about recruiting volunteers to help with the programme. My mouth twisted in a wry line as I listened to how easy it was going to be. *Hmmm, maybe in America, but to get unpaid volunteers at home? The words needle and haystack came to mind.*

I sat back and surreptitiously read my father's email reply. "Bossy. Love you, too. Dad x."

I stifled a giggle. So Rosemary was okay then.

The rest of the week flew by. It was such a peaceful campus nestled in the Berkshires, great for long walks after dinner to contemplate what I had learned that day. I went for my last evening stroll around the lake, my head cocked skywards, watching as an eagle soared above. I drank in the peacefulness. The silence was wonderful. For a moment, just a short moment, I felt like I didn't want to leave the serenity of the Option Institute and go back to real life, to dealing with

Rosemary's temper tantrums, desperately trying to juggle being a mother to a special kid, and being the sole breadwinner. *Life could be tough*, I thought. Suddenly I felt scared—scared to go home and face a mountain of responsibility. I was terrified to try in case I failed. I swallowed hard and took one last look at my beautiful surroundings. I would like to come back one day.

It was the final morning, and most people had already gone home, but some folks who were travelling long distances stayed the extra night. My case was packed, and I was enjoying a cuppa after breakfast. A young man in his twenties sat across from me. Our eyes met. I smiled, and he smiled back. I lifted my cup, and he let out a gasp.

'No! Don't drink that!'

I froze on the spot.

'Sorry! It's my fault. That coffee has been in the pot since yesterday. I forgot to change it this morning. It's going to taste awful. That's the regular coffee, isn't it?'

'Erm, no, it's tea.'

'Oh, thank goodness!'

'It certainly tastes alright to me!'

There was a pause.

'Are you a volunteer here?', I ventured. The whole week all our meals had been served up by smiling volunteers. I had become friendly with many of them, but I hadn't remembered meeting this young man until now.

'Was, but I've finished now. Thought I would pay it back before going home soon.'

'Where's home?'

'San Diego . . . Well actually, it's gonna be Los Angeles now. I gotta go and find an apartment in LA. I've got a new job. I start in a week.'

We got chatting. His name was Lou, and he had just graduated college as a journalist and had secured an internship at an LA newspaper. When I asked him what he had meant by volunteering so he could pay it back, it transpired his parents had run a Son-Rise Program for him from age two to age five. He had been completely non-verbal and severely autistic.

'Do you remember much about it?'

'Only a bit. I remember my playroom. I loved it there. Apparently, I would tantrum when it was time to come out! I remember my volunteers. I'm still in contact with some of them.'

'Well, you've certainly come a long way from there.'

'Yeah, pretty much. There are some traces of Asperger's left, but not much, nothing I'd call a problem. If anything, I can study for longer!'

'And do you remember what it felt like?'

'Sort of. Just the colours. Colours used to be so much brighter when I was little. I was very drawn to them. I would see bright colours where other people wouldn't really notice. And I remember spinning also. I used to spin myself around and around, and it made the colours spin, too. But that's all I can remember. So that's why I volunteered, to put a bit back again.' I was enthralled.

I was having an appropriate adult conversation with another adult. He had graduated from university and had his foot on the first rung of the career ladder. He flew from one side of America to the other by himself, could hold down a voluntary position, and look after himself just like any other young adult. There was nothing different or odd about him; he was just, "a regular guy" as the Americans would say.

Now *that's* the outcome I want for Rosemary!

Our conversation stayed with me on the train journey back to New York. I learned a lot that week at the Option Institute, but by far, the most prophetic moment had been my brief conversation with Lou that morning. Lou was living proof that autistic people can and do overcome their difficulties and lead typical lives. In a few years, maybe Rosemary and I could serve breakfast to new Son-Rise parents because we, too, wanted to pay it back. I really hoped this would be the case. I am so glad I had breakfast with Lou that morning, and I found myself feeling much less scared about the future.

Flying home, my reservations over my ability to help my child prove the clinicians wrong faded as the famous New York skyline faded into the distance. We were going to do this! I made myself a solemn promise that Rosemary and I would come back to New York to celebrate her sixteenth birthday. We were going to do the impossible. Rosemary was going to overcome her autism difficulties, just like Lou did. She would be independent, and she, too, would follow her dreams. Lou was a journalist. Well, I always said Rosemary would make a great nurse, didn't I?

CHAPTER 9

The Sun Keeps on Rising

When I got home from the States, Rosemary and I ran to each other and hugged tightly. No words, just clung onto each other, like we never wanted to be parted again. My parents were worn out from taking care of her for a full week. Rosemary's behaviour had been challenging, and she kicked her grandparents when she got frustrated. She loved them, but being away from me for a week was too much for her. I knew as I drove her back home that I couldn't leave her with my parents again like that. I had one chance to help her, and I was not going to screw it up. I knew all too well; I was putting a considerable amount of pressure on myself, but in my mind, there was no other path to take. That pressure would remain full-on for the next few years with inadequate periods of respite. That pressure would take an immense toll on my health.

Back home, Rosemary's Son-Rise Program was in full swing. The programme calls for a dedicated playroom, so I set about converting the garage into a suitable space. My brother-in-law was handy, so he started the ball rolling by insulating the roof and transforming the space into her new playroom whenever he could find the time. Rather than wait for the new area to be ready, we continued in the living room as before.

Have I mentioned how tiring it can be? Giving the three E's—energy, excitement, and enthusiasm—all the time could sure take the wind out of your sails. Our routine was pretty packed. I would get out of work around 5 pm, then it was time for dinner, then about three hours of Son-Rise play, then bed. We were both exhausted.

This had to work as I knew I wasn't going to get any second chances. Any research I had done suggested that the younger the child was when you began any therapy, the better the outcome. As Rosemary was fast approaching her seventh birthday, time was not on our side.

I sat down one evening at the kitchen table to prepare for the following day's play therapy. "Flexibility", I wrote. Flexibility wasn't her strongest attribute. I looked up the flexibility section of The Son-Rise Program Developmental Model. I chewed on my pencil for a minute then wrote, "Join for a while, then when I get the green light, we both turn into superheroes and fly to the moon." Okay, let's think of another. "Join for a while then when you get the green light, Barbie gets abducted by aliens." That'll do it.

Next: "Eye Contact." I decided on a game of hairdressers, and we could take turns guessing if the customer likes their hair by looking at their facial expressions in the mirror. We could always give Barbie an eighties perm in the process.

Okay, what next? I was on a roll. "Verbal Communication." My eye fell on the section about using figures of speech/colloquialisms during play. I scribbled down a few well-known idioms such as, "I feel as fit as a fiddle", and "I'm just pulling your leg". Done. I put my pencil down and stretched my tired muscles. This was the part of the day I enjoyed the most—the planning and direction which I wasn't half bad at.

My phone beeped. It was a text from Patsy setting up a meeting for the next day. I was so excited and had taken the day off work just to meet her. When trawling through the various Son-Rise videos online, I noticed one family's accents. They had taken their son out of nursery school and home-schooled him with The Son-Rise Program for several years, then placed him in school, where he blended in with the rest of the kids.

I was apprehensive about meeting her for coffee the next day, but there was no need; she was lovely. She was generous with her advice and didn't mind me taking notes as she chattered. It was great to have someone who understood my situation entirely.

'So, how is Oliver now?'

'Oh, great! He goes off to town with his friends most weekends. He's happy in school, too.'

'But he was completely non-verbal at the start, wasn't he?'

'Oh, yes, the speech therapist told me my son would never talk. You should have seen her face a year later when he bumped into her in the supermarket and apologised!'

I smiled and sipped my drink.

'And you know what his first word was? Bagheera! I was reading him The Jungle Book one night at bedtime when he pointed straight at it, saying it as clear as a bell!'

'You must have nearly died!'

'More like a heart attack! All that time he wasn't talking, he was actually teaching himself how to read. He could read before he could speak, and that's when we realised how intelligent he was.'

'And you took him out of nursery, didn't you?'

'Best thing we ever did. The nursery wasn't happy about it one bit, mind you. I got back from the Start-Up course, all fired up, took him out the very next day, and home-schooled him.'

Another home-school mum! How on earth do they do it?

'In fact, he only started school around the age of nine, and only for two hours a day. It wasn't until he was about eleven, maybe twelve years old that he went full time.'

I continued to scribble furiously.

'He's still got a few bits of autism left, but there's no comparison to how he started.'

First Lou, now Oliver. Both started with severe autism and were now blending in with their peers. They both still had autism, of course, but they had improved enough to lead ordinary lives. I wanted that for my Rosemary so much it hurt.

'Did you do the diet?'

'The what? Oh, the gluten and dairy thing? No, there was never any problem with food allergies. We did just Son-Rise for six years.'

'Oh, my God, that must have been tough!'

'Mmm . . . yes, but I had help. I didn't do it all myself. We had quite a few volunteers actually.'

'You managed to recruit volunteers?'

'Well, *paid* volunteers, yes. Just the going babysitting rates mind you. And all were girls. I was more comfortable with girls. We put an advert in the high school newsletter. We got loads of replies.' Her voice became earnest.

'Listen, Ruthangela, I had a husband and family to help out. You're on your own. You need to ask for help because if you try to do it all yourself, you'll burn out. It's too hard going.'

I nodded. She had a point.

'You can do this. I know you can. I can see the determination in your face, but you need to take some time for yourself. Get some volunteers on board, good ones.'

I mulled over Patsy's words, and with my renewed optimism, I arrived home and got to work designing the newspaper advert.

Volunteers Wanted

Are you silly and fun? Energetic and enthusiastic?
A big kid at heart?

Willing to learn valuable skills?

Babysitters required for play-based therapy sessions with a young child with autism.

No experience necessary. Just bags of energy, loads of enthusiasm, and an open mind.

On-going training and feedback will be provided.

Interested? Email for further details.

Pssst! Wallflowers and shrinking violets need not apply!

I waited for replies to come flooding in. When they didn't, I tried again, this time online for free. I reran the exact same advert again online, and I got some replies. One of the first was from a teenage girl living locally. Her name was Erin, and she was still at school, aspiring to a career in childcare. I rang her immediately. I needed to be sure she had the right kind of personality and to make doubly sure she knew what was expected of her.

'This isn't your typical babysitting gig now. There won't be any watching TV or doing your homework. It's going to be full-on. Call it babysitting on steroids!'

I started to explain how I had travelled to the USA to learn how to implement a play-based programme for my daughter and spoke of the progress she had made to date. Then I mentioned the importance of eye contact and the three E's.'

'Oh, are you talking about Son-Rise?'

'Yes, you know of it?'

'Yeah, I did that with a little boy a couple of years ago. He lived around the corner. They moved away, though, so I only did it for a few months. He was completely non-verbal and had no eye-contact. Your daughter sounds completely different, though.'

Someone else speaks my language! And she lives ten minutes away!

'I'd love to work with her. I used to play with Barbies when I was little, so I would love to play with Rosemary!'

Would someone pinch me, please?

For her first Son-Rise session, I had really just intended for Erin to observe me and to get an idea of how I joined with Rosemary. But after a few minutes, Erin had totally taken over, joining with Rosemary, encouraging more eye-contact. This girl was a natural. She was born with the three E's! I was beside myself with excitement. Very soon, Erin starting doing three sessions a week. Rosemary was delighted with her new best friend, and her little face just lit up when she saw her.

We plotted Rosemary's steady progress on The Son-Rise Program Developmental Model. Erin was in total agreement with me that the flexibility section was the area that required the most focus.

Rosemary's programme was gaining momentum now. I decided it was time to recruit more babysitters as Rosemary needed to be able to adapt to new situations and people. I made contact with other girls who had replied to the advert and found three more babysitters; Annie, Rebecca, and Heather. Annie was also a schoolgirl, Rebecca worked in a nursery, and Heather was a classroom assistant who worked with children with special needs. They, too, were naturally good at working the Son-Rise process with Rosemary.

I introduced each new babysitter one at a time, just like I had with Erin. Rosemary was shy at first with her new friends, even sitting with her back to Annie for the first hour. Annie then asked if she could play, too, and Rosemary obliged. By the end of the session, she was lifting her and twirling her about.

Six months into her Son-Rise Program, she was in love with her new routine. Now, she had four special people who played with her for hours on end. I can honestly say that this was one of the happiest periods of Rosemary's life to date. Yes, she was autistic, and she had language issues, but she was having so much fun!

My role was more planning and overseeing now, and to be honest, having suffered from a slipped disc, it had left me much less mobile than before. Lifting Rosemary up and swinging her about like her babysitters did was something I wasn't able to do anymore. I observed play and made notes, then sifted through the data. I plotted the progress against The Son-Rise Program Developmental Model, and each session was planned the evening before with quick check notes for her babysitters to scan as they went along.

Heather had arrived for her playdate, and I greeted her with enthusiasm. It certainly helped that I could nip out for an hour or two to get an errand done and, yes, even go to the hairdresser! Oh, freedom!

'Here's your notes for today, Helen. I thought you could incorporate idioms as you play, so I've written down a few examples you could shout out as you go, like, "that was a piece of cake" or "let's get our skates on," stuff like that, whatever fits the situation.'

Heather nodded and glanced over her cheat sheet as Rosemary grabbed her by the arm, pulling her into the living room to play.

'Helen! Play Supergirl with me! Please!

'Enjoy!'

I left them to it and went to the hair salon. Life was good!

I exhaled long and deep in the hairdresser's chair. I had a magazine and a cup of tea, I was in heaven. The hairdresser was talking nineteen to the dozen.

'Oh, your little girl goes to a special school, does she? Does she like it? Do you mind me asking what your daughter has?'

'She has autism.'

'Is she not able to talk then?'

'Oh, no, she is a little chatterbox. She has difficulties with . . .'

I stopped for a second. I was going to say her eye contact could be poor if she was feeling uncomfortable, that she adhered to rigid routines, was inflexible, talked about the same subjects, and watched the same DVDs over and over. But Rosemary had changed. She had made so much progress that by now, she was well established within Stage 4 of The Son-Rise Program Developmental Model. Her flexibility had improved significantly, and her eye contact was more or less that of a neurotypical child. She still had some difficulties associated with autism, though.

'. . . some day to day stuff', I concluded.

'So you must be in contact a lot with the school then? Aren't those special schools supposed to be very hands-on, always on the phone letting you know how the little bird is?'

In a word, no. No, they were not. In fact, communication from the school was rather perfunctory in nature. They used a daily information sheet that they checked off the activities they had done that day, with room for a brief comment at the bottom of the page, which was usually left blank.

On one occasion, there had been a message scribbled on the page, 'A child attempted to bite Rosemary in the playground today.'

When I asked Rosemary about it, her bottom lip quivered as she showed me the bite mark on her arm.

'Rosemary, what on earth happened?'

'Lucy did her biting on me!'

I had met this child in the supermarket before. She was easily twice the size of Rosemary. When I quizzed her further about it, it turned out it wasn't the first time that Lucy had inflicted injury upon her. I rang the school the next day and spoke to the teacher. 'Hello, Mrs Giles? Thank you for taking my call. It's about what happened yesterday.'

'Erm . . . yesterday?' She sounded vague.

'Yes, you wrote in Rosemary's folder that a child had attempted to bite her?'

'Oh, yeah, right, okay then.'

'Can I ask you, Mrs Giles, did a child attempt to bite Rosemary, or did she actually bite her?'

'Oh, I'm not sure; I wasn't there.'

'But you wrote the note, didn't you?'

Silence.

'Mrs Giles, did the child attempt to bite Rosemary, or did she actually bite her?'

'Erm . . . erm . . .'

Mrs Giles apparently didn't like the question.

'I've spoken to Rosemary about this, so I already know the answer. Did the child actually bite Rosemary, or was it just an attempt to bite her?'

'Erm . . . erm . . .'

'I've seen the bite mark on Rosemary's arm, Mrs Giles.'

'She actually bit her.'

'Thank you. Is it the first time something like this has happened?'

'Erm . . . erm . . .'

'Has it happened before?'

'I don't think it has actually . . .'

'Mrs Giles, I already know the answer to this one as well. Has it happened before?'

'Yes, it has.'

'Is the child in question called Lucy?'

'I'm not at liberty to . . .'

'Is the little girl called Lucy, Mrs Giles?'

'Yes.'

'And Lucy has been targeting Rosemary for some time? Is that right?'

'Well . . . yes.'

'I see. Tell me, what is being done to protect my daughter?'

The most frustrating thing about that phone conversation with Rosemary's teacher was that I had to drag the truth out of her. By the end of the conversation, however, things were much more positive. We had agreed that the school would draft up a plan of action in terms of distracting this little girl Lucy away from Rosemary, and what the agreed actions should be if Rosemary were hurt again by her. Mrs Giles said she would have the action plan typed up and sent out to me within the next couple of days.

'Great, thank you. I'll look forward to receiving that. Oh, and now that I'm thinking of it, if there are any further situations like this, would you ensure that I am told about it, please? It's not very often that I see any sort of feedback written in Rosemary's information folder; the daily sheets are usually left blank, or with just a picture of a smiley face drawn on.'

'Oh, right.'

'It would really help a lot if I could get daily feedback about how well Rosemary is doing. She gets the bus to school and back, so I'm not able to catch up with you any other way, Mrs Giles.'

'Okay, I'll have feedback in the folder each day for you.'

'Thank you.'

This had happened a few weeks ago, and I hadn't been made aware of any further incidents either by the school or Rosemary when I quizzed her. *No news is good news*, I thought. I flicked through my magazine and smiled as the hairdresser chittered on.

I let my mind wander. *What if the school has noticed the progress Rosemary has made?* I imagined the scenario in my head, the teacher looking stunned, explaining what a transformation she had seen in my child,

'What's the secret, Mizzsssscccch Bernadette? I simply can't get over how much progress she has made! What's the secret?'

I enjoyed my little make-believe movie for a while. Actually, now that I was thinking about it, didn't I have a meeting coming up quite soon at the school anyway? I fumbled in my handbag and checked my schedule on my phone. I had a parent-teacher annual review meeting the following week. I'd never been to one of these meetings before, even though she had been there for two years. Funny that it's supposed to be annual. I shrugged and returned to my daydream. 'She's a completely different child, Mizzsssscccch Bernadette. You must have done a lot of work with her. What's the secret?'

I sipped my tea while I enjoyed my little escape from reality. I was a contented cat.

CHAPTER 10

Back Down to Earth with a Bump

My annual review meeting with Rosemary's teacher was the final one of the day. School had finished, and most of the staff had already gone home. The last time I was at the school, Rosemary had just been diagnosed, and my awareness of autism was practically non-existent. At least by now, I had read enough books and had amassed adequate knowledge of the condition to hold my own in a conversation with the experts in a special school. I had certainly achieved expert status with regards to my own child's autism—that was undeniable. I wondered just how much Rosemary's teachers had observed. Her flexibility had improved, as had her concentration. Her eye contact was what would be considered normal for a child her age. She was able to tell me how she was feeling, something she had never been able to do before. I couldn't wait to hear about how much Rosemary had improved from the teacher's perspective. I shifted about in my chair, eager to get started. Having come prepared, I had sprayed a handkerchief with perfume for an emergency sniff, if required.

'Mizzsssscccch Bernadette. Thank you so much for waiting. Would you like to come in, please?'

Rosemary's teeny-weeny teacher sat down on a pupil's seat and invited me to do the same. I went to sit down where indicated and missed. After a scramble, I managed to plonk my ample rear end onto the kiddy-chair and waited, knees under my chin. She looked entirely comfortable with the seating arrangement, whereas I must have looked like Alice in Wonderland. I looked around the room for the bottle labelled, "Drink Me". No such luck.

'I wonder if we could begin by me asking a few questions if that's alright, Mizzsssscccch Bernadette.'

'Sure, no problem.'

'Do you ever read to your daughter?'

What a strange question.

'Oh, yes, of course I do. She gets a bedtime story each night. Actually, our bedtime routine has changed slightly. She writes down how she is feeling in her Feelings Journal every night, then she gets a story of her choosing, after which is time for sleep.'

Mrs Giles looked surprised.

'Thank you. And do you ever discipline your daughter?'

What a weird question.

'Excuse me? Discipline my daughter? Well, if she has been naughty, I usually remove a privilege such as television time. But more often, I use the time out method.'

'How many minutes?'

'Seven.'

'Seven? So precise?'

'Yes, of course, it's supposed to be one minute for every year of the child's life, isn't it? With her attention difficulties, I would not be happy in it being any longer.'

'And that's your method of discipline?' she asked flatly.

'Yes, it is.' I retorted a little too firmly.

'And does it work?'

'Of course, it does. If it didn't, I wouldn't use it.'

'Hmmm. I have been having discipline issues with Rosemary in class.'

'You have?'

'And it would appear that it stems from a lack of discipline at home, and I'm not convinced that you are employing any real method of correction . . .'

'Excuse me, let me just clarify what you are saying here. Are you suggesting time outs and removal of privileges are not enough? Surely, you are not suggesting anything more forceful, Mrs Giles? I sincerely hope not.'

'She really does lack discipline Mizzsssscccch Bernadette.'

'I am not going to smack my child, Mrs Giles.'

'She needs discipline. She's naughty.'

'She's autistic.'

'No, she's autistic, and she is also naughty. They are two separate things.'

Someone hasn't been applying their TEACCH principles.

'But Mrs Giles, surely you must be aware that, as the teacher of the class, you are the one in charge, and you are the disciplinarian. The world and its wives know that for young children, you need to correct a child immediately after the behaviour happens. You should know that. I fail to see how my confronting my daughter at six o'clock in the evening over something that happened at nine that morning would be of any benefit.'

Silence.

Okay, time for a game of fishing.

'Mrs Giles, what are the TEACCH methods for discipline?'

It was Mrs Giles's turn to shift uncomfortably in her miniature seat. She cleared her throat.

'You said you use TEACCH methods within the classroom, Mrs Giles. Which of the TEACCH strategies do you use?'

Dinky doll bristled.

Busted!

She changed the subject.

'Last week, Rosemary refused to do her colouring in, so I let her have a few sweets and told her that if she behaved herself, she could have some more, but her behaviour only got worse. She wouldn't sit in her seat, was running around, being disruptive, argumentative . . .'

'Are you saying you gave my daughter sugar, then wondered why she became hyper?'

Realisation spread across her face. Her cheeks flushed. She changed the subject again. 'And she won't sit still during circle time either. She likes to do the same things all the time. Even the other day . . .'

'Sorry, let me stop you there. You're talking about my child having difficulty joining in group activities and preferring to do the same thing over and over, aren't you? That's autism, Mrs Giles. That's what autistic kids do. Your class is specifically for autistic children, and you are a teacher of autistic pupils. Are you complaining that one of your pupils is showing autistic behaviours?'

Her face reddened further.

'Erm, the reason why I asked you about reading is that Rosemary seems to avoid reading at all costs. She will use an array of distraction techniques, answering back, running away, anything to avoid standing up beside me and reading a book Mizzsssscccch Bernadette.'

This did not make any sense. Rosemary *loved* reading with me at home.

'And her maths work isn't much better', she went on. 'She'll avoid doing sums with me, too. I don't think she has managed any simple addition or subtraction at all, in fact.'

Now, this was an even bigger shock. If anyone was a human calculator, Rosemary was. She could thank my father for that gene.

'What do you mean? Rosemary can add and subtract as accurately as I can.'

Thumbelina looked genuinely shocked.

'But . . . but, she can't! I mean, she won't! She won't do any sums for me at all!'

'I don't know what's going on here Mrs Giles, but Rosemary will happily sit and do basic calculations for me at home. Very happily, and very easily. Very easily, indeed.'

'But she can't!'

'Actually, she *can*.'

A pause.

She shot me a dismissive look as she added, 'Well anyway, it's not just English and Maths. In fact, I have not taught any of the curriculum whatsoever to Rosemary in the past eighteen months, at least.'

Whhhhaaaaatttt?

She dropped the bomb as cool as ice. She was laid back, very matter of fact. For once, I was almost speechless. Almost.

'Pardon?'

'Yes, I have not delivered any curriculum teaching to Rosemary for the past eighteen months or so . . .'

'Excuse me? Did you say you have not taught my daughter anything for the past eighteen months? Did I hear you right?'

'I just haven't found a way to get Rosemary to co-operate with me.' She shrugged.

'You haven't been teaching my daughter *anything*? For the past eighteen months?'

'Mizzsssscccch Bernadette . . .' she rolled her eyes.

'Nothing at all?'

'No.'

Mrs Giles shook her head briefly and looked at me as if to say, '*and your problem is?*'

'And you left it *eighteen months* before you decided to tell me? Why did you leave it so long? Talk about letting it snowball!'

'I wouldn't actually refer to it as snowballing, I would call it . . . Rosemary's *problem*. She likes to get her own way a lot; it's almost as if she . . .' Mrs Giles stopped abruptly and gasped as if in a light-bulb moment. 'It's like she needs to control the situation!'

She looked chuffed with her little revelation and sat back in her mini seat, lifting her heels off the floor.

'Are you referring to high functioning or Asperger's kids and their compulsion to control, Mrs Giles?'

A pause.

'That's because the two things go together.'

Silence.

Did she hear me?

'The two things go together?', I ventured.

Surely this woman understood what I just said? She must do!

Nothing.

Okay, I'll re-phrase.

'Controlling behaviour and Asperger's?'

Silence.

'They go together like fish and chips! Surely you knew that?'

Blank stare.

Oh, my God, she doesn't!

'Please tell me you knew that.'

Blank stare.

'You didn't know that?'

I put my head in my hands.

'Oh, my God, she doesn't know that!'

You said that out loud, you idiot!

Mrs Giles must have decided it was in her best interests to steer the conversation elsewhere yet again. In retrospect, I couldn't have blamed her, as there I was, head in hands, making little effort to conceal my incredulity at her lack of basic autism knowledge. Talk about a picture saying a thousand words.

'Mizzssssccccch Bernadette, I understand Rosemary has a diagnosis of high functioning autism, is that right?'

'Yes, she does.' I muttered.

'Hmmm. I'm not sure she was fully diagnosed, Mizzssssccccch Bernadette. I think that in addition to her autism, she has . . . oh, dear, I've forgotten the name of it now. Erm, Opposing Disruptive . . . No, that's not it, erm Opposite Deviant . . . Defiant . . . No, that's not it either. Oh, it's on the tip of my tongue Mizzssssccccch Bernadette. I think she should be reassessed for Opulent Disorder . . . erm, oh, dear, what's it called now?'

I am so not hearing this!

'Oh, the terminology escapes me now. Erm, some people abbreviate it to D. O. D.? Erm . . . O. D. O.?'

Okay, enough.

'Are you referring to Oppositional Defiant Disorder, Mrs Giles?'

'Yes! That's it! Opposite . . . erm . . . Opposite . . . thingy . . . yes! In addition to her autism, I think she also has Opposite . . . erm . . . Opposite . . .'

I never did suffer fools gladly.

'Hmmm, see, I'm going to be really honest with you, Mrs Giles.'

I leaned forward into her personal space and steepled my fingers. My voice was low and even.

'If you are going to try your hand at diagnosing a child, you really need to be able to pronounce the condition, as well as having a basic working knowledge of it.'

'I see.', she squeaked.

Talk about having a face like a slapped arse! She looked like she wanted to punch me. Pity, her aim was only knee-high.

I hadn't finished. My little girl had made tremendous strides in her Son-Rise Program, and I was proud of her. I was not going to let some teacher who pretended to know more than she did try to divert the spotlight from her own failings onto me.

'She's nothing like this with me, Mrs Giles. Not by a country mile. My child will read and do maths for me until the cows come home. In fact, it would appear that my daughter has learned more at my kitchen table in the past six weeks than she has in your school for the past two years. What on earth have you been doing all this time?'

Silence.

'There is obviously something about her school environment that makes her uncomfortable. Like the classroom walls, for instance.'

'The walls?'

'Yes, the walls.'

Blank stare.

'Don't you think they are too visually stimulating for an autistic child?'

Blanker stare.

'Look around you, Mrs Giles. Every inch of wall is covered in luminous pink, luminous orange laminated posters, and you've got drawings and 3D art everywhere. There are snakes hanging down from the ceiling behind you. There are rain clouds and suns hanging down by the window. The desks and chairs are multi-coloured. The whole room looks like it's on acid, Mrs Giles. My teeth are on edge just sitting here, and I'm neurotypical. Don't you know about calm, uncluttered surroundings for children on the spectrum?'

'But . . . but all the rooms are like this. This is a typical classroom, Mizzsssscccch Bernadette.'

'So, you are saying that neither you nor the entire school for that matter, have any knowledge of autism-friendly classrooms? Is that right?'

'There is nothing wrong with the classroom Mizzsssscccch Bernadette!'

'But this is the autism unit of a special school! It has been designed specifically for autistic children, and yet, it is sensory overload, Mrs Giles!'

'It's what?'

'Please tell me Mrs Giles, have you not heard of sensory overload? Overstimulation?'

Silence.

I buried my head in my hands a second time.

'Oh, Lord, she doesn't know that either!' I sobbed.

You said it out loud again, Ruthangela!

'This is basic stuff, Mrs Giles! Basic stuff!'

The red mist had truly descended. I was ranting now, and I wasn't going to stop anytime soon. That educational psychologist had well and truly over-sold this school to me.

'You are supposed to be the expert here, not me! You're supposed to be appropriately qualified and trained! This is supposed to be a special school! Your unit is the autism unit, specifically designed for autistic children, and yet, I'm having to impart basic information about the autistic spectrum to you! It should be the other way around!'

Mrs Giles looked hacked off, her mouth set in a firm line, her petite arms and legs crossed.

'Are you honestly saying you know nothing about autistic children needing a distraction-free environment to learn?'

'I'm not going to answer you Mizzsssscccch Bernadette.'

'Too right, you're not going to answer me because you don't even understand the question in the first place!'

'Mizzsssscccch Bernadette, if we could just discuss your daughter, please. Her behaviour in class can be very difficult. She tries to monopolise my time, leaving me with less time for the other pupils.'

'How do you mean monopolise your time? There are four adults and six children in the class!'

'Well, she asks me a lot of questions.'

'Like what?'

'Well, like what we are going to do next, or what's for lunch, or if it's time to use the soft play area. She even asks me questions when she already knows the answer. She asks me the same questions several times a day, every single day Mizzsssscccch Bernadette. And quite frankly, it gets on my nerves!'

Now I don't know about you, but whenever I've been at the movies, and the actor suddenly receives some shocking or disturbing news, the camera quickly pans onto him, while the audience is surrounded by the sound of a plane losing altitude and plummeting towards the ground. Well, there was no camera in the room at the time. I checked, because for a fleeting moment, I could have sworn I was on *Candid Camera*, but as God is my witness, I really did hear the sound of the plane crashing, and it was loud!

'She gets on your nerves?'

Will that plane ever stop?

'My daughter gets on your nerves?'

'Yes, your daughter's behaviour gets on my nerves! Yes, it does!'

'My daughter gets on your nerves when she asks you questions, does she? And what do you say to her?'

'Well, sometimes I tell her I'm not going to answer any of her silly questions, but I usually just ignore her!'

'She does that because she's uncomfortable. She's obviously nervous about something, so she will seek reassurance from you. She came to you for comfort, and you told her to sling her hook. And you wonder why she's got an attitude towards you?'

Has that bloody plane not crashed yet?

'But it's relentless, Mizzsssscccch Bernadette! It's daily, and I find it very frustrating!'

'A word of advice Mrs Giles, when there are children around, and special children at that, you've got to behave like you're Mary Poppins even when you feel like Cruella De Vil.'

'There's no need to speak like that, Mizzsssscccch Bernadette.'

You're damn lucky I didn't make any reference to Snow White's roommates, you short-arsed little prick!

'And may I suggest that the next time my daughter gets on your nerves by asking you a question, heaven forbid, that you leave the room, count to ten, then walk back in. If you can't *be* professional Mrs Giles, you can at least *pretend* that you are.'

Okay, you've said enough now—time to go before you dig yourself deeper.

'Now *you* are getting on *my* nerves Mrs Giles, so *I* am going to take a deep breath and walk out of here', I said as I scrambled up out of my mini-chair. Somehow, I managed to put one foot in front of the other and make my way out of the classroom even though my whole body was shaking. I don't think I have ever been as angry in my whole life. Yes, I was totally condescending towards this so-called special needs teacher, but by God, she deserved it. I got to the door and turned around.

'And my name is Miss Bernadette. Miss. M. I. S. S. If you were unsure of my marital status, goodness knows why you think it's relevant; all you had to do was ask.'

'I'm sorry, Mizzsssscccch, I mean *Miss* Bernadette. I wasn't sure . . . I didn't know . . . I didn't know . . .'

'Yeah, well, what you don't know could fill a warehouse!'

I just about managed to resist the temptation to slam the door behind me as I left, the sound of the plane in distress still ringing in my ears.

Better start looking for a new school Ruthangela.

Instead of the customary song, I must thank the lovely Mr Sigmund Freud for the complimentary light aircraft sound effects, which were a reference to my hopes and dreams crashing all around me. At that very moment, all my hopes and dreams did come crashing down. I had whipped myself up into a frenzy with Rosemary's Son-Rise Program, having allowed myself to believe she could possibly achieve a relatively *normal* life. Unrealistic dreams? Probably. And by golly, was I coming back down to earth with a bump!

I ventilated as I got into the car. Surely a special needs teacher is a vocation! These teachers are supposed to care! This woman didn't give a damn about my daughter—it's just a day job for her! What she knew about autism could be written on the back of a postage stamp!

I remembered her last words to me when I visited the school before, promising to teach Rosemary the curriculum. What a liar! She had no intention of keeping her word!

Later that evening in the car, as we drove in silence, I studied Rosemary's reflection in the rear-view mirror when we stopped at the lights. She looked so sweet. I just couldn't imagine her being so difficult at school and not wanting to learn anything at all. She didn't want to read? This did not sound like my daughter at all. Rosemary *loved* reading with me at home.

'Rosemary, honey?'

'Yeah?'

'Do you like reading books at school, dear?'

'No.'

'You never told me, pet.'

'Uh-huh.'

'You know the way you like doing hard sums with me?'

'Yeah.'

'Don't you like doing sums for Mrs Giles?'

'No.'

'And reading? Don't you like reading for Mrs Giles?'

'No.'

'Why don't you like doing any work for your teacher darling?'

'Because I do have to be going up to her desk and doing my standing beside her.'

'Is that not okay?'

'No.'

'Why not?'

'She does smell.'

'Of what?'

She studied her reflection in the window as she deliberated, then turned and fixed her beautiful blue eyes on me before she delivered her answer with aplomb.

'Cabbage.'

Well if you don't ask, you'll never know.

I'd like to say that I woke up the next morning feeling philosophical about the school meeting. I didn't. I was still as angry as hell.

She hadn't even flinched when she told me that Rosemary got on her nerves. What a thing to say about a child! In her mind, it was entirely acceptable to have such disdain for a pupil, and inadequate knowledge of the autistic spectrum, or complete lack thereof!

Maybe the meeting at the school had only served to spur me on even more. I *did* dare to dream of the possibility that my daughter would eventually become completely independent. *I did!* And nobody was going to stop me, especially not some pint-sized naysayer who knew very little about very little.

Thank you, Mrs Giles. You gave me a kick up the rear end and made me even more determined to help my daughter. For this, I thank you.

When I had composed myself, I rang the Local Education Authority, and I spoke to someone about what had happened. Talk about saying it like it is. He was so honest with me, brutally honest, in fact. Suffice to say, my eyes were well and truly opened during that conversation.

I told him what had transpired the day before and how I had lost all trust in my daughter's teacher, explaining how I was not prepared to keep my daughter in a school like that a day longer than I had to. He listened to me and agreed with my decision that the best course of action was to remove Rosemary from the school and place her elsewhere. We also agreed that the teacher's attitude towards my daughter was so inappropriate that it could not go unreported. To pursue the matter, I would need to make a formal complaint to the school board, but before that, I would need to go through the appropriate channels and give the school principal her place and have a meeting with her. At the very least, it would give her the opportunity to try to put some things right; it was only fair.

'Don't expect anyone to hold their hands up and admit fault now, but do make the complaint. You must do it. I can assure you it won't go unnoticed, and conversations will be behind closed doors. And copy me in on the letter when you send it.' His candid advice was refreshing, to say the least. I got the distinct impression he had been there and bought the tee-shirt when it came to the poor standards of special education teachers.

A few days later, Rosemary alighted the bus, her little face swollen with tears.

'Rosemary, honey! What on earth is wrong?'

'Lucy did pushed me in the playground, and I felled down and hurted myself!'

Not again! I checked her information folder. Nothing. Not a word. I sat her down and got her to tell me everything blow by blow; what exactly happened, the name of the teacher who witnessed it, rhyme, chapter, and verse.

I picked up the phone again.

'Mrs Giles, were there any incidents at school today?'

'No', came the clipped reply.

'Nothing at all?'

'No.'

'Was Rosemary pushed in the playground today?'

'No.'

Her monosyllabic answers told me this was going to be hard work.

'Mrs Giles. Rosemary has just told me that Lucy pushed her over in the playground.'

'No, that didn't happen Mizzsssscccch Bernadette.'

'Have you spoken with Mrs Walker?'

'Mrs Walker?'

'Yes, Mrs Walker witnessed the incident and cleaned Rosemary's wound for her. Yet, there is no mention of it in her information folder.'

'Oh, . . . right.'

'Would you mind speaking to Mrs Walker and calling me back, please?'

I could hear a loud sigh coming down the receiver.

'Okay, Mizzsssscccch Bernadette', and the line clicked dead. She didn't call me back.

I left it to the next day and called her again.

'Yes, it would appear there may have been an incident of sorts' was her reply.

'Of sorts? I'm sorry I'm not with you. Was there or wasn't there an incident Mrs Giles?'

'There was.'

'But nothing was recorded on the daily information sheet.'

Silence.

'Do you know why?'

'There wasn't time.'

'And was it Lucy, again?'

Silence.

'Mrs Giles, was it Lucy who hurt Rosemary?'

'*Yesssssssss*', came the retort from behind her clenched teeth.

'And tell me, did Rosemary retaliate in any way?'

'No.'

'And what are you doing to protect Rosemary?'

'We're implementing the action plan we discussed.'

'Okay, thank you, Mrs Giles. Can you please ensure that I am kept informed from now on?'

'*Yessssssss*', she hissed.

'Thank you. As you'll remember, when we last spoke about Lucy, we agreed that the school would . . .'

Click! The line went dead again.

I shook my head. No point in getting annoyed with her since soon she would be an unfortunate chapter in Rosemary's history. I busied myself with making a fuss over Rosemary and cooking her favourite dinner. She must be scared stiff of this kid, Lucy.

'Rosemary, pet?'

'Yeah?'

'Do you think you might be able to stay away from Lucy in the playground?'

'But what if Lucy does come and finding me?'

'You'll need to tell a teacher then. Do you think you can do that?'

'Erm . . . yeah.'

She didn't sound entirely confident.

'You know biting and hitting isn't allowed, don't you?'

'Hitting is bad.'

'Yes, it's a very bad thing to do indeed. But, it's going to be alright, darling. I'm going to speak to the school principal tomorrow about it. You don't need to worry about a thing. Just try to stay away from her if you can.'

'Okay, mummy.'

After bath time, she got dressed in her pyjamas and dressing gown, settled on the sofa with me, and started reading her book, a happy little girl.

Reading at home had always been an enjoyable past-time together. Up until then, I had believed the school was progressively taking her through the reading stages. After I had put her to bed, I googled a few of her book titles, only to find out that she was about eighteen months behind peer average reading age. I exhaled heavily. I was going to have to do something about that, too. The past week had been stressful; first was the disappointment of the teacher not commenting on any improvement in her social skills, then the bombshells she had dropped, and more recently, her evasive actions over Rosemary being bullied in the playground. I had started looking for a new school for Rosemary with renewed determination to get it right this time. I was feeling stressed, and I needed a break, a chance to clear my mind. My go-to method of dealing with stress at that time was typically comfort-eating. If I wasn't in the mood for that, or I was already too full, I would turn my attention to cleaning out cupboards and wardrobes instead. However, they'd all had a major going over after the meeting with my daughter's school teacher, and had all been scrubbed and reorganised within an inch of their lives. I stood with my hands on my hips. I wondered what other chores I could tackle. My eyes lifted skywards, 'A-ha! The attic!' I flexed my muscles and climbed the ladder.

I started with the big stuff: tables, lamps, and suitcases. Now what? I opened the boxes "for filing," old bank statements, bills, brochures, most of which could be shredded. I opened another box and found old scripts that I flicked through. Nothing seemed familiar to me, and judging by the yellowed paper, these were pretty old scripts at that. I looked at the cover, "Robin Hood and His Merry Men". Then it dawned on me that these were my mother's old scripts, not mine.

I sat down cross-legged. I used to love going to the theatre as a child, especially at Christmas, because my mum was always the principal boy in the pantomime. Jacket dresses, fishnets, and six-inch heels, yes, the good old days of panto! When men were . . . erm, women, and old ladies were . . . well, men. I remembered that Robin Hood production, my mum looking leggy and fabulous in her green Robin Hood costume. I remember her sword fight with the Sheriff of Rottingham, jumping up on the table, and fighting off assailants with a few kung-fu kicks. You know, sometimes, mums can really rock, and my mum certainly kicked ass when she was in panto. I skimmed through the scenes, giggling at the corny lines, but what was this next scene? I read the handwritten notes. It looked like an extra scene had been shoehorned in at the last minute, most likely to buy the backstage crew some time to change the set. I traced my mother's scriptwriting with my finger, "Camp Military Drill. Boys. 3 minutes. Costume change, check props, and standby stage left." I sat back as the memories came flooding in. It was a sort of Christmassy send-up of *Monty Python's*, "Camp Military Drill"[14], consisting of eight camp soldiers flouncing up and down the stage, limp-wristed, forming a kick line. I remembered this routine even though I must have been very young when I saw it. I recalled it was incredibly funny at the time. I was far too young to appreciate that all they were doing was sending up gay men. *Monty Python's* humour might have been ground-breaking in the seventies, but comic genius aside, a scene devised solely to poke fun at gay men just wouldn't fly nowadays for its inappropriateness. I read down through the rest of the script.

"Oooh, get her! Whoops!
I've got your number ducky
You couldn't afford me, dear . . ."

I let out a snort as my memories came flooding back.

"Two! Three! Four!
Whoops! Don't look now, girls.
The major's just minced in . . ."

I must have been up in the attic for over an hour, reading the script from the overture to the finale, looking at my mother's notations, and reminiscing. My mother was a real glamour puss back then. She was also a triple threat; she could act, sing, and dance. I was so in awe of her that at the end of every performance, I would rush backstage to greet her and the rest of the cast. My eyes would dart around the dressing room, looking at the feather boas, sequins, wigs, makeup. Everything and everyone was just so fabulous and showbizzy. I was hooked, even then.

I grabbed a few things to take to the dump and climbed down into the hall again. My clothes and hair were filthy, so I had no qualms wiping my even filthier hands down my tee-shirt. At least, I had the next day off work for my meeting with the school principal. Also, I could finish up in the attic another day, so that I might take myself off for a nice quiet lunch, followed by a walk in the park—a little me-time.

CHAPTER 11

How's the School Hunt Going?

I sat in the school reception area. I was a couple of minutes early for my meeting and could still feel the same eerie atmosphere. Whoever thought a school could be so unnaturally silent? I shuddered. I'd never met the principal properly face to face before. Actually, now that I thought of it, the school principal was on maternity leave, and the vice principal had stepped in for a while before she went off on maternity leave, too. I racked my brains. Hadn't the Board of Governors asked some retired geography teacher to fill in for the next few months? I remembered reading something in the parents' newsletter, but I'd forgotten his name. Oh, well, I'd never met him either. At least, he wouldn't be filling out a maternity leave form any time soon.

Okay, Ruthangela, just go through the motions and give the man his due. He'll probably want to make Rosemary feel safe for the remainder of her time here, at the very least.

I waited some more.

I read *Homes and Gardens* from cover to cover.

Eventually, I heard a door close at the far end of the corridor and saw a figure coming towards me, but he wasn't walking, he was . . . I could only think of one word . . . *mincing*. He minced towards me, pigeon-toed with short strides, the only thing missing was his jazz hands.

He continued to slink towards me. His heels clicked a steady rhythm along the corridor. *One Two Three Four.*

Five! Six! Seven! Eight!

"Oooh, get her! Whoops!

I've got your number ducky.

You couldn't afford me, dear. Two three . . ."

Oh, for God's sake, not now!

'Mith Bernadette?'

'Yes?'

'I'm Mithta Jeffwee', he spoke with a lisp.

He swept his ring finger along his tweezed brow. I watched his hand begin to fall by his side then, in total horror, continued to watch as he proceeded to place his hand on his . . .

No! Don't do it! Don't put your hand on your . . .

He placed his hand on his hip, balletic fingers splayed.

Oh, my God. He didn't just do that! Please tell me he didn't do that!

'Erm . . . thank you for seeing me Mr . . .'

'I am not here to talk to you, Mith Bernadette. You did not wing the offithe to confirm your attendanth, therefore I canthelled our meeting today.'

He turned to the grumpy receptionist. 'Amanda, would you show Mith Bernadette the way out pleathe? Goodbye.'

'I beg your pardon? Did you cancel our meeting? And you didn't bother to tell me? What's going on?'

'What's *not* going on is any meeting, Mith Bernadette.'

Now, in the past, if I had found myself in a situation such as this, I would have been easily roused. Short fuse? Moi? That morning, his unexpected cancellation didn't bother me too much—not immediately anyway. In my mind, I suppose I was elsewhere. I had moved on in a way because I was already making plans to visit other schools. So, I was past being angry with the school in spite of what had transpired. That morning, I was simply going through the motions so I could check it off as done. I wasn't angry; I was just inconvenienced, for now. The anger came a bit later.

I stood up, hands on my hips.

For goodness sake, you're mimicking him now!

I quickly released my arms.

There's the door Miss Bernadette.'

Now wait a minute, this guy is just being prat. What was his issue with me?

'Why are you so angry with me, Mr Jeffrey? Should it not be the other way around? Your school has failed my daughter. By rights, *I* should be the angry party, not you.'

'You wrote to the school board. I have nothing to say to you.'

'Oh, so *that's* why! You're taking it personally because I went over your head. Is that what the problem is?'

'You . . . you . . . you wrote to the board!'

The receptionist made a sharp exit, which was the only time I ever witnessed that woman doing anything at speed. I turned my attention back to the simpering specimen in front of me.

'I see, I understand your irritation now. Yes, I did write to the board. And if a teacher told you that your kid got on their nerves, you'd be writing to the board, too!'

'Mrs Giles is a dedicated and experienced teacher, and she has my full backing and support.'

Now I was starting to get annoyed.

'She does, does she? So, are you saying my daughter gets on your nerves, too?'

He pressed his fingers to his décolleté and recoiled, presumably in disgust, at my suggestion.

Oh, come off it! Nobody is that camp!

"Don't come the brigadier bit with us, dear,
We all know where you've been, you military fairy!"

'I'm not going to comment on anything Mrs Giles did or did not say.'

"Whoops, don't look now girls.
The major's just minced in . . ."

Oh, stop it, please!

'It's okay, Mr Jeffrey. I just thought it was right to give you your place and let you try to make some reparations. But as you've said, I've written to the board, so it's probably best they manage the situation until Rosemary's departure.'

'Manage the situation? What do you mean?'

'I mean her safety, Mr Jeffrey. A much bigger child has been picking on her in the playground, biting her, pushing her . . .'

His face took on a quizzical look.

'Sorry, I thought you knew?'

Silence.

'Were you not aware of that?'

'I can manage the situation perfectly well. I am the principal, you know.'

Go on, Ruthangela, he's left it wide open!

'But you're not, are you?'

My camp friend looked puzzled.

'You're not the principal, nor are you the acting principal. You're the "acting acting principal," aren't you?'

He glowered at me.

Back of the net!

'But how can you act like a school's "acting acting principal" when you're not even aware of what's going on? The teaching staff has not been reporting the incidents to me either, Mr Jeffrey. More often than not, the daily information sheet is left entirely blank.'

'That's because nothing happened. Rosemary has probably just been making it all up!'

'Oh, has she now? And did she make up the bite mark on her arm? What about Mrs Walker? Was she making that up, too? Are the pair of them in it together?'

He blinked furiously.

Oh, please! Is guy for real, fluttering his eyelashes?

I wanted to throw the biggest left uppercut to this man's face so badly. Actually, make that two uppercuts; the right for my gay friends and the left from Rosemary and I. Nobody is naturally that camp. Nobody! Gay, straight, or otherwise. This guy was taking the mickey, big time.

I took a deep breath; there was no point in arguing with the man. I decided to make my point and leave.

'It's entirely up to you, Mr Jeffrey. If you're unable to ensure my daughter's safety within the grounds of the school, then I will have to rely on the police instead!'

Now I didn't think what I just said had been particularly inflammatory, but apparently, it was.

'If you call the police on me, then . . . then . . . then I will call social services on you!' He sprayed.

Inflammatory or not, his rebuke was uncalled for. That was *waaayyy* below the belt.

'Really, Mr Jeffrey? You would call social services on me? On what grounds?'

'Th . . . tha . . . that's all I have to say, Miss Bernadette! Goodbye!'

He turned and slinked back down the corridor, his pace much brisker than before.

Quick march! One! Two! Three! Four!

If you think you're getting away with that, you've another thing coming, mate.

I followed him.

Five! Six! Seven! Eight!

'Are you seriously saying you would make a false report to social services? Would you do that, Mr Jeffrey?'

'This conversation is over, Miss Bernadette! Please close the door on your way out!', he shouted over his shoulder.

No way, mate. You're not going to have the final word with me, you pompous idiot!

'No, Mr Jeffrey, this conversation is not over! Now would you please tell me, for the record, why you might place a call to social services about me? What have I done? Stood up for my daughter? Stood up to you? Since when was that a cause for concern?'

He continued down towards his office. I hadn't finished. I continued my pursuit of him.

'Actually, now that I'm thinking about it, refusing to provide a child with an education might be adequate grounds, perhaps I should call them instead?'

His pace slowed.

Finish the job, Ruthangela! Finish it!

'Or, maybe I should just call the newspapers.'

And mic drop!

He stopped abruptly, mid-slink, and turned towards me. He looked like he wanted to shoot me.

Well, if being assertive is a crime, fire away, little man, fire away.

'Mr Jeffrey, I am not leaving until you explain yourself. I have all day.'

A pause.

'I'm going to ask you one more time, Mr Jeffrey, what grounds would you have to call social services?'

Silence.

'It was a straight forward question, Mr Jeffrey, a simple answer will suffice.'

'I . . . I . . .'

'Yes?'

'I . . . I wouldn't . . . erm . . .'

He shifted uncomfortably. His face reddened.

'Erm, I wouldn't . . . actually.'

I raised an eyebrow inviting him to elaborate.

'I wouldn't call them Miss Bernadette. I said it . . . I just said it to . . . erm . . . to . . . erm.'

'To win?' I interjected.

He paused. His face softened as he slumped ever so slightly.

'I shouldn't have said it. I'm sorry.'

Okay, he admitted it. Fair do's.

'Okay, Mr Jeffrey, thank you for your honesty.'

Now it was my turn to turn my back on him. He had chucked me out of his school after all, so it was time to go. I opened the door and stood for a second.

'So, I take it you are aware I am removing my child from your school Mr Jeffrey? Would you do me a favour and please keep her out of harm's way until then?'

He nodded.

I walked out of that school and never looked back.

Well, at least the school kept one promise to me.

My head was reeling as I got back into my car. Did that really happen? Surely not! I shook my head as I drove along. First, there was the Amazing Four Foot Woman, then the Queen of Pink Christmases! What's next? The Incredible Bearded Lady?

I must have imagined it all—his walk and his mannerisms. I was short-sighted and wore glasses for driving, going to the theatre, things like that. I wasn't wearing my glasses at the time, so maybe I imagined the way he held himself? No, that wasn't possible because he was right up close to me when he started with all those hand gestures and eyelash fluttering business. Oh, my God, he really does act like that! There couldn't possibly be any other explanation for it. Despite his unpleasantness, it made no sense whatsoever why he might put on a show for the sake of it. The man was simply as camp as a row of tents. Well, I'll be damned!

He did, however, admit to threatening me just for the sake of it, which took some humility on his part, and probably explained why I wasn't feeling any animosity towards him. But how on earth could all this have happened? The whole scenario seemed so unbelievable, ludicrous in fact, but it truly happened. So why?

Was it my fault? Had I rubbed the acting acting principal, and the teacher up the wrong way? I know I could be assertive when it came to fighting for Rosemary, but maybe I was a little bit too fierce. Maybe I unleashed my inner Cruella De Vil too readily.

The acting acting principal was an asshole, and the teacher was an asshole, too, but in earnest, so was I. I was a great big loud-mouthed, shooting from the hip, asshole. Yep. Nothing like a large helping of home truth.

Shit, Ruthangela, you really bring out the worst in folks, don't you?

I lodged my formal complaint with the school Board of Governors, then focussed my attention on sourcing a new school for my daughter and arranged school visits. I remembered my conversation with the Education Authority. "Choose the next school very carefully, Miss Bernadette, and be smart about it. You should also have a second school in your back pocket just in case."

Sound advice it was. I attended the Board of Governors meeting and went through the motions. Given my warning from the Education Authority, I didn't expect anything ground-breaking to happen. My complaint must have been listened to because after that day, there wasn't a squeak out of Lucy, and there was always some sort of news in Rosemary's daily information sheet. Oh, and I nearly forgot, Mrs Giles never set foot in Rosemary's class ever again. Result!

Rosemary's teacher had been replaced for the remainder of the term, and Rosemary and her new educator got on well. Her reading had started to improve, and she was beginning to show steady progress in her maths, spellings, and handwriting. Her daily information sheets always had a positive message written in, well except for one entry which read, "Rosemary informed the classroom assistant this morning that she was barking up the wrong tree."

So the idioms work paid off then.

A couple of weeks later, there was a letter in Rosemary's schoolbag addressed to me. *Hmmm, this couldn't possibly be an apology from the board, could it?* I opened the letter and skimmed the contents.

". . . we wish to inform you . . . Rosemary has been assessed . . . moderate learning disability . . . IQ of 65."

I dropped the letter and grabbed the kitchen table to steady myself.

Rosemary had autism, language delay, *and* a learning disability.

I read it again.

Rosemary had autism, language delay, *and* a learning disability!

No way! Absolutely no way! Rosemary is a clever girl. This couldn't possibly be accurate! I knew I was right. My gut instinct was speaking to me, loud and clear. It had told me that Rosemary *did* have autism the weekend before she got her autism diagnosis, and now it was telling me to ignore this secondary diagnosis.

I rang my parents.

'There is no question of that child having an IQ of sixty-five. Not in a million years!', My father said.

'We all know she's a smart little girl Ruthangela, her maths is better than mine!' My mum volunteered.

'Ignore the letter', my father suggested. 'The sooner she's out of that place, the better. How's the new school hunt going?'

I had visited several schools, and I liked one, in particular, a little school in the countryside with classes so small that two school years were amalgamated into one class. The school principal was a charming lady, and so was the teacher. They both were very focussed on the individual child. However, there was something about it that left me feeling flat, and I couldn't quite put my finger on it. Perhaps it was best to have a Plan B in my pocket as the Education Authority guy had said.

I didn't have a second choice yet, but I had appointments to visit the few remaining schools in the area the next day.

As events would pan out, one of them stood out for all the right reasons. It was much nearer to home, and it had a good reputation. It was a mainstream school with a unit attached that catered to children with a range of special needs, be it moderate learning disability, autism, ADHD, or hearing disability.

I arrived in the bright reception area, and the receptionist even appeared genuinely pleased to see a prospective new parent! How refreshing! Within seconds, the school principal greeted me.

He was a busy man, friendly but business-like. He even wore the school tie himself. It was clear he was very proud of his school.

'The special unit is just here', he said. 'I made sure it was slap bang in the middle of the school building because we have an inclusive ethos here. Children in the unit integrate with the rest of the school in every way, including school choir and football practice. Each child joins their mainstream peer class every afternoon as well.' I was introduced to the class teacher, and when the tour finished, we sat in his office. 'This is a decision you've got to get right', he said. 'The school you choose will be your daughter's second home for the next few years, and she's got to be happy in whatever environment you choose.'

I nodded. This man *got* me.

'And the objective of the unit is to get the child out of the unit and into the mainstream.'

This man *really* got me.

This is the right school for my daughter. This is the one.

I rang the Education Authority and asked for the girl that had been working on Rosemary's case, making the preparations for her to move to the little country school.

'Hello? It's Ruthangela Bernadette here, Rosemary's mummy.'

'Hello Miss Bernadette, what can I do for you?'
'You're going to kill me!'
'I am?'
'Yes, after what I'm about to tell you, you will kill me!'
'Okay, try me.'
'I've changed my mind.'
'About what?'
'I've changed my mind about Rosemary's school. I've just come from another school, and I've been completely sold on it.'

'Alright then, we can change it. What's the name of the school?'

Rosemary went along with me to see the school herself the following week. We met the principal again, her teacher, and the special needs coordinator. Rosemary loved the school, too, but with three new people all making such a fuss of her, she was very shy and self-conscious.

'Do you like my school, Rosemary?', asked the principal.
Rosemary nodded.
'What do you like the best?'
'The playground', she whispered.
'So, do you think you would like to come to school here in September, then?'
'Yes, please!' She smiled.

This time I signed the paperwork with a flourish and a handshake instead of a woozy uneasiness.

CHAPTER 12

Unteachable

With summer fast approaching and Rosemary's days in her old school well and truly numbered, I spotted an advert in the local newspaper about a company called Top of the Class that provided private tuition over the holidays. *Well, if the mountain will not come to Mohammed.* What better way to help Rosemary regain some of the ground she lost when her education was stopped?

I set up an assessment appointment for her. The assessor chatted briefly with Rosemary before setting her up at the computer to test her mathematics and reading. My back was getting stiff again, so rather than sit and wait, I decided to walk around the office, taking in my surroundings. The large metal clock ticked loudly on the wall as I paced about the room.

I found myself drawn to a framed picture on the wall of the tutor, wader clad, fishing rod strapped to his back, and grinning from ear to ear while holding a freshly caught salmon. I stood and admired it for a while until another picture stole my attention. On his desk was another picture of him with his wife and two kids, or so I guessed them to be. It was a rather old fashioned picture of the family unit, all smiling, arms draped around each other in front of a brown, swirly-smudgy background. I smiled at the picture; they looked so happy. My eyes fell on his full black moustache.

Eighties fashion, you have a lot to answer for. I thought to myself.

'What an adorable little girl Miss Bernadette!'

I jumped and turned around.

'Thank you.'

'I'm sorry, but I don't think we are going to be able to help you. What age is Rosemary? Seven and a half? She might as well have been a five-year-old sitting in front of me Miss Bernadette, and her reading ability is too far behind. It's affecting her maths because she can't read the questions. Your daughter is unteachable. I'm sorry.'

He must have seen the look of alarm on my face because he quickly tried to soften the blow.

'Oh, I'm sorry that didn't come out awfully well. It's just that we're not set up here to cater to your daughter's needs. We are the ones who have let Rosemary down, not the other way around.'

I blinked back the tears.

'Feel free to bring her back in six months and prove me wrong. Please do.'

'Oh, okay, then.', I mumbled.

'Will I come here again and play with the computer mummy?', Rosemary asked as we left Top of the Class.

'No, love.'

'But why?'

'Because you're too clever, that's why.'

CHAPTER 13

Food Intolerances

I'll show him! I thought to myself. I was determined to prove all the naysayers wrong, and with a renewed sense of energy, I set about getting Rosemary's reading up to par. I ignored the letter about Rosemary having a learning disability and trawled Amazon for staged reading books.

It was the summer holiday period, so every day after work, I collected Rosemary from the nursery, and after dinner, we concentrated on her reading. We got through a book every two days at first, and by the end of the summer, she was reading and understanding one book that was several stages higher per day.

After dinner one evening, we sat down to read again. But as she began reading, Rosemary started fidgeting, rubbing her ears, and couldn't concentrate.

'Are you okay, Rosemary pet?'

'I do feel funny.'

'Funny? In what way?'

'Wriggly.'

She didn't look good. Both her ears were roaring red. She used to get like this every now and then in the past, and the doctor's helpline would say something must have disagreed with her, and would advise that I give her an antihistamine. The usual questions would ensue, like whether or not I had changed the washing powder recently. It wasn't just her ears though; she would also get an angry-looking rash over her bottom, which would disappear after a few hours. I used to think that her school had been using too strong a cleaner on the toilet seats, and Rosemary had sensitive skin like mine. I joined the dots. My thoughts went back to The Son-Rise Program and what Kym had whispered to me during a session talking about the GFCF diet.

"Lots of kids are on the diet, even if they're not allergic. It helps a lot."

A discussion had broken out about some kids on the spectrum also being allergic or highly intolerant to gluten and dairy. I looked at the dinner plates still on the table. Spaghetti Carbonara—gluten in the pasta and dairy in the sauce, I wonder . . .

I scoured the internet and found a kinesiologist a few miles away. I'd never been to this sort of professional before, so I decided that Rosemary should be tested blind. I didn't mention any specific foodstuffs of concern.

The appointment lasted a couple of hours. By the end of it, Rosemary was diagnosed as being highly intolerant, bordering on allergic, to: gluten, cow's milk, corn, soy, and cantaloupe melon.

My daughter was actually intolerant to dairy and gluten, amongst others, so my decision to go gluten-free, casein-free (GFCF) with her was really thrust upon me rather than a carefully pondered choice. I was advised to remove dairy first from her diet, as it was easier, then to remove gluten when I had got the hang of the whole dairy thing.

We went shopping, and for the first time in years, I scrutinised the ingredients label of everything before I bought it. Some foods that I would never have imagined would ever contain milk did, thus were placed back on the shelf. My initial fear that Rosemary wouldn't like the new food turned out to be unfounded as she happily ate her gluten, corn, soy, and dairy-free breakfast the next morning without a word. *This is going surprisingly well.* I told the nursery not to give her any food or snacks from now on since I would be supplying all of that. Unfortunately, the fact that they were no longer feeding her wasn't reflected in their monthly bill. After a few weeks, I removed the rest of the offending foodstuffs. Now going gluten-free was much more complicated than going dairy-free. I had to watch for certain words on packaging like malt, rye, barley, spelt, and a whole gamut of foods. Then when I was sure the food was free from dairy and gluten, I would realise it was full of corn or soy. And if it was free from all aforementioned ingredients, I could bet my bottom dollar it was crammed full of sugar. *Aaarrghhhhh!*

Shopping soon became a lengthy and challenging operation. To say my learning curve was steep was an understatement. I was also very aware that whilst I needed to remove the foods that disagreed with her, I also had to ensure her diet wasn't too high in carbohydrates and refined sugar. I was becoming a real food snob, at least where Rosemary was concerned. I just ate what was cheap and available whenever I got the chance, but for Rosemary, if the label contained more than five ingredients, I wasn't interested. If it contained MSG or any artificial ingredients, it was not making its way into my shopping trolley. Too much sugar? No way was it getting past me. Can't pronounce it? Then she definitely can't eat it. I modelled her eating habits after my grandmother when she cooked for her family. Nothing was labelled as *organic* in those days because everything was. She made bread each day, so I did likewise. She cooked basic, plain meals for her children, and so did I. A typical meal for us would be organic meat, potatoes, plenty of vegetables, and gravy made with the meat juices. I ended up spending more time in the kitchen than ever.

I soon got used to the new schedule of going to work, then Rosemary's reading, Son-Rise, and cooking. Rosemary's eczema started to disappear, and her ears also returned to their natural colour. She was doing great work reading at home with me every day. Her Son-Rise work with her babysitters was also going extremely well. In fact, she was now entering Stage 5 of The Son-Rise Program Developmental Model, and I was getting excited about her progress.

I skipped off to work each day, boring my workmates by lecturing them on the benefits of their children eating organic foods and reducing sugar intake. I cut out GFCF recipes from magazines and pinned them to noticeboards. I was tired but happy.

My phone rang.

'Hello, Miss Bernadette? It's Sharon from the nursery here.'

Rosemary attended her nursery during the school holidays.

'Hi, Sharon. How are you?'

'Erm, not good. Ruthangela, I don't know how to say it, but Rosemary's . . . she's . . . she's just gone mad!'

'Mad? What do you mean?'

'She's gone into total meltdown! She's been hitting out at the children and staff here. You're going to have to come and get her. We can't cope!'

From the racket I could hear in the background, I knew she was serious. I jumped into my car, trying to keep myself calm as I drove to the nursery.

Please, no! Not this all over again! I clicked on the radio for a distraction.

"Her name was Lola, she was a showgirl.
With yellow feathers in her hair and a dress cut down to there."[15]

I am going to have to seriously reconsider my choice of radio station.

I hit the off button and concentrated on my breathing until I got there, instead. Anything to remain calm.

You would not believe the scene that greeted me when I got there! There were toys strewn around the room, exhausted-looking staff, and Rosemary, the poor mite, looked terrified. Her face was red and swollen with crying so much, and she was physically shaking when I picked her up.

'It's alright; Mummy's here.'

'Mummy! Mummy!'

'It's alright, darling. I'm here.'

I held her tight and could feel her little heart pounding against mine.

What on earth had happened? I had no idea. Had something happened at the nursery? What had caused this ruckus?

Taking long deep breaths, I bundled her into the car and started off home. Stopping at the traffic lights, I recalled the conversation about GFCF diets at The Son-Rise Program, and the revelation came like a bolt of lightning. *She's a crack addict! She hasn't had any gluten, dairy, or sugar in her diet, and she's craving them. She's feeling the effects of withdrawal!*

Someone needs time off work now! When I got home, I picked up the phone and explained the situation to my manager. I had a new boss by then, a female boss with kids of her own. Lately at work, there had been a management incentive for staff to choose to work part-time, term time, or even to take a sabbatical, which probably swung her decision so easily. In the end, we decided I would take the month of August off work unpaid. I rang the nursery and said that Rosemary would not be back for a month. Pity, they still charged me for it.

Her withdrawal period lasted almost three weeks. She had meltdowns and tantrums, but bit by bit, my happy, mischievous little girl came back again.

Looking back at this short period in my life, I realise it was difficult but also worth it. I was blessed that other parents had gone through it before I did and wrote about it. I found I was able to cope because I knew what the problem was. Thank goodness for the internet! It was also around this time that I decided that when I returned to work, it would only be on a part-time basis so I could devote more time to my daughter. She was younger than her years and needed to have her mummy about more often. Also, I got to indulge myself by spending more time with my special pal.

August also had its pleasant moments. We spent a lot of time doing Son-Rise and reading more books. We spent every single waking moment together and then slept in the same bed each night. We already had a very close bond, but we became even closer during that time.

I looked at the calendar on the fridge one morning. Only a few more days until Rosemary started her new school.

'Rosemary honey, we're going to go out soon. We've to get your new school uniform today! Are you excited?'

'Yeah!'

'What do you want to do when we get back later? We could go to the park if you like, or you could play with your Barbies. You haven't played with them in a while, have you?'

'Want park. Don't like Barbie.'

'Yes, of course, we can go . . . Sorry Rosemary, what did you say?'

'Don't like Barbie. Barbie is for babies.'

'Is she really?'

'Yeah.'

'But you have so much Barbie stuff Rosemary. Don't you like any of it?'

'No.'

'None of it at all?'

'No.'

'Well, what do you want to do with all your Barbies then?

She pondered a moment.

'Throw them in the bin. Don't like Barbie anymores.'

Had I heard her correctly?

True to form when we got home later that morning, Rosemary helped me pack up the car with all her Barbie paraphernalia to take to the charity shop. We filled the car to bursting, seats flattened. It took three journeys. Oh, and I *accidentally* stood on Barbie a few times during the Barbie extermination exercise. Well, she asked for it, the little bitch.

My father wasn't entirely convinced, 'What all of them? All of her Barbies? Every last one?'

'Every last one, Dad.'

'Oh!'

Silence as he digested the information.

'Why didn't you sell them on eBay instead? You could have put an extension on the house with the money. How is the work in the garage coming along? Her playroom should be ready by now.'

'Yeah, just a bit of painting to do, and it'll be ready.'

'Does Rosemary want to speak to her Nana and Grandad?'

'Rosemary, dear! Do you want to talk on the phone?'

I watched her as she entered the room and took the phone from me. She wandered about, phone to her ear, giggling, chattering away to her grandparents, telling them what a big girl she was now, and asking them when they were coming to see her. My gaze turned to her bare feet as she padded about. Did my eyes deceive me? Had she stopped toe-walking? Now that I came to think of it, the last time I saw her flapping her hands was weeks ago as well! I cupped my face with my hands as I realised how far she had come. My daughter was in Stage 5 of The Son-Rise Program Developmental Model and had lost all of her stims! I couldn't remember when she last asked the same questions over and over or wanted to discuss the same topic all the time. I examined the DVDs on the shelf, the ones she used to watch ad nauseam, and ran my finger over the top. Dust! The DVDs were beginning to gather dust because they had been on the shelf, unused, for so long. And as of today, she had no interest in Barbie whatsoever! I jumped off the sofa and grabbed Rosemary in my arms and swung her around.

'Wheeeee! Look at Rosemary! Who is the best girl in the world? Who is a big clever girl? Rosemary is!

'Is everything alright?' I could hear my father's voice coming down the phone receiver.

'Yes! Everything is great! I'll call you back tonight, Dad, when she's asleep!'

We danced around the living room, not wanting that afternoon ever to stop. I was beyond delighted. It was all starting to come together—her Son-Rise, her diet, her new school, and our at-home reading programme. Rosemary was on her way now!

CHAPTER 14

Home-School

The first day of Rosemary's new school dawned. I was nervously excited, and Rosemary was, too. She looked so cute in her uniform. I took her into her classroom, where both the teacher and assistant were very welcoming, saying it was fine for me to leave her with them. So, I did. I took one last look over my shoulder, and there was my little girl sitting all by herself, playing with one of the toys. She looked so small and lost. I wanted to run back and hug her, but I knew it was best just to leave her be. She was in good hands.

I kept busy that day to stop myself from fretting and was first at the school gates later that afternoon to collect her. I saw the school principal, and he waved and came over to me.

'Did you know Rosemary is a super footballer?'

'She is?'

'Yes, she was a bit shy in the playground, being her first day at school. She didn't seem to want to talk to me at all, so I didn't talk to her either, I just kicked the ball to her. Then she kicked it back, and soon we were having a very enjoyable game of football. She had a great first day. Great! She has made friends and has played beautifully with them. Her teacher is very pleased with her. She seems happy, Miss Bernadette, very happy indeed.'

I was relieved. Not only was Rosemary a happy little bunny at her new school, but the school principal also seemed to really get her. It was as if he instinctively knew how to handle her. She didn't want to talk to him? No problem. So he didn't talk to her either.

Rosemary's little face lit up when she saw me, running to jump into my arms.

'Mummy, I do have friends!' she exclaimed.

I covered her in kisses. I was so happy for her, and at that moment, I knew I had made the right decision to change her school.

About six weeks later was the parent-teacher meeting at school. I was given my appointment time and waited nervously in the school reception. The last time I had a progress meeting at my daughter's school, it had all gone rather pear-shaped, to say the least. I pressed my hand down on my leg to stop it from shaking. I heard my name called and looked up. It was the school principal, and he was smiling. I followed him into the office.

'Thank you for coming, Miss Bernadette. We like to have a meeting with parents twice a year to keep up to date, so we'll have another meeting towards the end of the school year.'

Wow! Two meetings a year? Now I'm no mathematician, but I'm pretty sure that beats one meeting every two years in her last place!

I was reintroduced to the special needs co-ordinator and her class teacher. I smiled and took a deep breath.

'Well, Rosemary has been doing great these past few weeks, just great! But . . .'

I knew there was going to be a "but!" There's always a "but!" I steadied myself to receive the blow.

'But there's something I need to double-check with you.'

'Yes?'

'This is a report from Rosemary's old school. Here's where they've assessed her reading ability at the end of the school year. Is that correct?'

'Yes, she was at that reading stage back in June.'

The three of them exchanged glances.

'Right then . . . It's just that Rosemary's reading ability was tested last week, and her current reading ability is within the expected range for her age peers.'

'So . . . she's caught up then?'

'Yes, it would appear that she's caught up over a year's worth of reading during the summer, Miss Bernadette. I take it that was your influence?'

'Yes, it was.'

'Well, whatever you're doing, Miss Bernadette, keep doing it!'

Did he just say that? Did he really? Had she caught up? Yes, she had! I just about managed to stop myself from jumping up and down in my seat.

The rest of the meeting was positive. She had made friends at school and had settled in nicely.

'Our primary concern is her language ability. It's the one thing that will keep her back, so Rosemary will be assessed in the next couple of weeks by the speech and language therapist, and she'll make contact with you to discuss the type of support she will provide.'

'I'll look forward to it. Yes, Rosemary's speech really does need work. Well, thank you all for your time.'

I stood up and shook hands with everyone. We were all smiling. This had never happened before.

I didn't walk out of the school; I gave my superhero cape an almighty whoosh and flew out of the school gates. I swear, I did.

Rosemary was reading at the mainstream level! Perhaps now I could begin to support her in other ways, so I decided to include some mathematics as well. I used to think that home-school mums were some kind of super human creatures! Well, maybe I was a super mum! Didn't I have a super child?

I hit Amazon like a woman possessed, buying all sorts of maths workbooks. I signed up for some home-school mathematics websites and got busy planning her at home schedule. Before I knew it, I had devised a full-blown home education programme for Rosemary.

Home educator? Moi? Who'd have thought it?

Rosemary enjoyed her new routine as she now had more variety to her sessions with me. I know I am biased when it comes to Rosemary, but I can safely say that I couldn't have asked for a better student. She was eager, she worked hard, and above all, we had fun! We played maths games in the car, while we are out walking, and during bath time. We still kept up her reading, but at a more leisurely pace. I really had no clue about how to address her speech and language difficulties, though, best to leave that to the experts! As predicted, my phone rang a couple of weeks later, and it was the Speech and Language Department.

'Hello, is that Miss Bernadette?'

'Yes, it is.'

'Hello! It's Miss Davies here. Sarah Davies, Speech and Language Department. I thought I would give you a ring to tell you about the work I will be doing with Rosemary this year. I understand one of my colleagues visited the school and assessed Rosemary recently?'

'Oh, yes, that's right.'

'Yes, I'm sorry I didn't do the assessment myself as I will be the one doing all the work with her. However, looking at her assessment report here, she has a severe language delay, so I'm going to recommend a block of speech and language sessions for Rosemary. '

'Oh, great, thank you.'

'And I will be working on her expressive and receptive language difficulties.'

'Oh, that's good, so that's speech therapy for the school year then? How often a week will that be?'

'What? No, it's one session every second week Miss Bernadette.'

'Oh, right, okay. Never mind, it's not so bad because at least I can be working with her between sessions then.'

'Well yes, but it's not a year, it's a block.'

'A block? What's a block?'

'A block covers a twelve-week period Miss Bernadette.'

'What? Only twelve sessions?'

'No, six.'

'Six? Did I hear you right? Did you just say six sessions?'

'Yes, you *did* hear me right.' There was a hint of annoyance in her voice.

'And how long is a session?'

'Twenty minutes.'

'Sorry, just let me recap here Miss Davies. You're recommending Rosemary gets just two hours' worth of speech and language therapy for the entire school year. Is that correct?'

'Yes, that *is* correct.'

'Two hours?'

'Yes.'

'And you think that's adequate, do you?'

'It's standard.'

'That's not what I asked you. I asked if you considered it adequate for her needs.'

'It's what the Education Authority will implement.'

'But the school principal said that Rosemary's language understanding was the one thing that was going to hold her back.'

'It's all I can offer, Miss Bernadette.'

'Right then!'

'I'm sensing a little opposition here, Miss Bernadette.'

You bet your ass you are.

'This is like . . .' I began.

'Like?'

'Like needing a Ferrari and being offered a Fiat!'

'I'm sorry, did you just compare me to a car, Miss Bernadette?'

Actually, a pair of roller skates would be more like it.

'Rosemary's progress to date has been quite phenomenal, Miss Davies. All it took was a little focus and hard work, and her progress has been across the board with her reading, maths, and now more recently, with her friendship skills. I see no reason why her progress with speech and language would be any different, but it would appear by offering her only two hours' worth of intervention, she's not going to get a chance.'

Miss Davies' voice became sterner.

'Look, Miss Bernadette. Rosemary will always have difficulties throughout her life. She'll always struggle, you know, with language in particular. And any child on the spectrum will always be a poor learner because of their poor eye contact and . . .'

'And did my daughter have poor eye contact during the assessment?'

'Well, of course, she had a poor eye . . . oh, let me see . . . erm, I'm not sure . . . let me just fetch the notes.'

I heard the frantic rustle of papers, then a pause.

'Miss Bernadette? Sorry to keep you there. I just had a look at the notes taken, and actually, Rosemary sustained good eye contact throughout the session.'

'Yes, I thought she might.'

'Your child may have good eye contact, but you can't expect me to wave my magic wand and fix her language issues for her. I can't do that, and to be honest, it would be unrealistic of you to expect too much progress.'

'Why do you think it's so unlikely?' I asked.

'Miss Bernadette! You need to manage your expectations of Rosemary! She will always have difficulties in life, no matter what anyone does!'

'Have you met her?'

There was a brief pause.

'No, I haven't met her, but . . .'

'And yet you're prepared to automatically write her off, even though you've never met her?'

Awkward silence.

'If you set the bar low, as you very clearly have, you're going to get exactly that—minimal improvement. Talk about giving up before you've already started!'

Maybe it's time you shut your mouth, Ruthangela?

'You say she'll never achieve anything because you're *ensuring* she doesn't. You're right, Miss Davies, she won't achieve much because you've already made up your mind that she won't!'

Okay, shut up now!

'If I had taken the same attitude as you, Rosemary wouldn't have covered over a year's worth of reading over the summer, would she?'

'Actually, I'm sensing some hostility here, Miss Bernadette.'

'You can call it what you like, but I prefer to call it tenacity and positivity, Miss Davies. You should try it sometime.'

I hung up.

Gobby? Moi?

Okay, Ruthangela, you'll have to add speech and language to the home programme now.

CHAPTER 15

My Kid's Doing Great, Not So Sure About Me

I looked at the phone I just slammed down on the counter. *Why, oh why did I have to open my mouth and let everything spill out like that? God, I hate myself!*

At that moment, a familiar feeling came over me—a feeling I had experienced many times before. I felt so totally and utterly alone. I was grateful that my daughter's new school seemed to suit her much better, but if I wanted to help my daughter, it pretty much boiled down to my efforts and mine alone. If I wanted my daughter to catch up academically, it was up to me. If I wanted her language to improve, that was entirely up to me, too—nobody else.

I chose not to believe Miss Davies that day. I am so glad I didn't, because if I had given into her pessimism, Rosemary would not be where she is today. I chose not to believe the private tutor either. Rosemary was certainly not unteachable, not even close. I chose not to believe Rosemary's old teacher in the special school who neither knew nor wanted to know how to teach autistic children. I chose not to believe Rosemary's old acting school principal because, let's face it, you just can't take a tutu-wearing clown seriously, no matter how hard you try. Okay, he wasn't actually wearing a tutu or a red nose for that matter, but let's not split hairs. I chose not to believe Rosemary had an IQ of 65; I knew she was much smarter than that. Why was I the only one who could see the potential in my child? Why couldn't the so-called professionals see it?

It was the most isolating feeling in the world.

It's not as if I could have talked through my frustrations with a therapist or life coach. No, that would never work. I imagined how the scenario might pan out, seeing myself draped over the therapist's couch, ice pack clamped to my forehead as I spew forth my problems whilst he sits, listening intently to my inane drivel. He does, of course, have the obligatory half spectacles, elbow pads, and heavy European accent.

'Thank you for seeing me, Dr Van Helsing. I've come to talk about how stressed I am. I'm a single working mother who is in the process of helping her daughter overcome her difficulties with autism, language delay, and learning disability. She's doing really well, but I feel overwhelmed and alone because nobody understands what I'm going through. If I try to talk about it, folks just give me a blank stare.'

I look up from the couch to see the therapist staring blankly at me.

Well, I did say it would never work.

I knew that if Rosemary and I were going to survive this, I was going to have to take as good care of myself as I did for my daughter, which was something I hadn't been doing. I put Rosemary first every time, neglecting my own needs. It was great for Rosemary, but not so great for me.

Remember, my mechanism for dealing with my stress was to either go on a cleaning frenzy or to overeat. Food numbed my emotions. I went into an almost zombie-like state, guzzling some cheap, sugar-laden substance, entering an alternative universe for a few minutes where no thoughts entered my mind. I just chewed and swallowed, chewed and swallowed, quietly, and serenely. I felt nothing whilst living in my alternative world. Afterward, I hated myself. I had gained so much weight to the extent that my joints hurt, and my back stiffened. Every morning, I woke up with severe back pain. By focussing all my efforts on Rosemary, I had lost myself completely. My love was a one-way street. If I could like myself just a little bit, that would be a start. My focus on Rosemary was unrelenting, but when it came to looking after myself, I didn't give it a second thought.

I sat myself down in front of my computer and went to the Son-Rise Facebook group and typed out a post,

"Hello, Son-Rise people. Can I lean on you all for some support? I am a single mum to a beautiful little girl with autism. Progress has been phenomenal, to the point where we are almost *there*. But, nobody ever told me how big a toll it would take on my own mental health. The highs of travelling this road are dizzying, and the lows are devastating. When my daughter first got diagnosed, we received no support, nothing at all. Nada. Wouldn't it be great if each kid could get a qualified nanny to babysit once a month to let an overworked, overstressed mum have a break? I am mentally and emotionally exhausted, but where can I turn to for help? A shrink? And one that understands Son-Rise? Yeah right. Like that's going to happen. My kid is doing great, and I am so thankful for that. But her progress comes at a price, and I'm paying with my emotional stability. I am broke, but the bills keep on coming. Amazon Books are laughing all the way to the bank, thanks to me! Yes, my kid is doing great, but I am definitely not. Anyone in the same boat?

Thank you.

Ruthangela, a Son-Rise Mum who hugged trees in the Berkshires once."

I sat and watched the post for a while—nothing. I hoped I wouldn't feel the wrath of parents berating me for being so negative when my child was doing so well, and their kid still wasn't speaking! I braced myself for the backlash. Yet still nothing.

I shrugged. Serves me right, nobody wants to listen to an old moan. I turned off the pc and shuffled into the kitchen. Rosemary was due home from school any minute, and I had to prepare her organic, gluten-free, dairy-free, corn-free, soy-free, melon-free, sugar-free evening meal from scratch.

Unable to sleep that night, I crept back downstairs and logged onto Facebook. I scrolled down to my post, and there, sitting below, were countless replies, all positive. Everyone who posted felt just like I did. Tears rolled down my cheeks as I read all the messages of comfort. Tears of gratitude, tears of relief that these people really got me. Tears that my peers accepted me. Tears of joy. Tears of hope.

What's the first thing you do when you fall off a horse? You get right back up again. So, I got back up.

I heaved my hulking torso off the chair and went out into the hall. I paused at the bottom of the stairs. Perhaps I should weigh myself? When I finally retired for the night, I did so in the knowledge that I tipped the scales at over fifteen stones.

CHAPTER 16

Negativity Is Kryptonite

The phone call with the speech and language therapist set the scene for the next couple of years for Rosemary and I. It was a case of grit your teeth and dig deep.

By now, she had graduated her Son-Rise Program. My brother in law downed tools and announced with a flourish that the Son-Rise garage-playroom was finished and ready for business! Rosemary progressed so quickly that she finished all her Son-Rise work before her playroom was ready! He sounded somewhat confused when I thanked him profusely for his work on the garage and commented on what a lovely gym it was going to be.

Rosemary was catching up academically now, but her language understanding and friendship skills needed a lot of work. I had worked out that Rosemary was not learning by assimilation like neurotypical children do. Any skills that she lacked had to be learned. For instance, I realised she didn't understand the meaning of the words *thick* and *thin*. Such basic words! Surely a child who had already celebrated her eighth birthday should have known these words? She didn't.

So now, after her much-loved-but-no-longer-required Son-Rise Program was put to bed with a fond kiss to the forehead, the home education phase was well and *truly* launched.

Me? A home-school mum? Every day when Rosemary got home from school, she'd have dinner, then homework, then home education time, and you know what? We both loved it!

I was the first person to notice her improvements whilst others didn't notice a thing. Let me make you a promise. Are you listening? You will be first to see the progress in your child. After a while, others will begin to notice. I promise you; they will. If you take care of your child's diet, their Son-Rise Program, their language, and their education, your child will respond. You can do it. She can do it. Believe in yourself. Believe in your child. If others don't believe in you, that's their problem, not yours.

There's a phenomenon about crabs in a bucket[16]. If you put one crab in a bucket, it will manage to crawl its way out of it in search of a better life. It is perfectly capable of doing so by itself. But if you put more than one crab in a bucket, the others will see the first one trying to get out and will use their pincers to drag it back down again. It's a case of 'If I can't have it, neither can you.' Let me tell you folks; crabs are everywhere. Learn to recognise a crab when you see one. Your crab might be a teacher, a clinician or therapist, a neighbour or friend, anyone in fact. Don't let them grab you or your child and bring either of you down. Just focus on your goals, irrespective of how much the crabs roll their eyes, clearly know more than you do, manage your expectations, urge you to be realistic, or whatever rhetoric they choose to employ. Do not listen to them. They only speak crab, and crab is a foreign language to you and I. Their negativity is pure kryptonite for superheroes. I learned my crab handling skills the hard way. I shot from the hip when I would have been better off keeping schtum. I made enemies because I didn't hold back in telling them exactly what I thought of them. In some cases, it was very much deserved, but I didn't have to be so honest. Dealing with crabs calls for specific skills, and I'd like to think I've honed them over the years after a pretty appalling start. So, here are my top tips for dealing with crabs (the bucket variety—for any other kind, please consult your GP).

Tip # 1: Just because it's true doesn't mean you should say it.

Think of some of my conversations in the past with some educators and clinicians, and this should be pretty much self-explanatory.

Tip # 2: Crabs are so negative because they know nothing else.

Crabs say the most negative things about your child because that's all they see around them. They have limited time and resources, and they are only able to give a child a fraction of what they really need, and the result? Failure. That's all they see year after year. So, when a crab tells you that they're not actually setting the bar low, that you need a healthy dose of reality, and to stop expecting miracles, that's because they've never seen anything bordering upon miraculous in all their working years. That's where you come in. You can either do the job yourself or pay a good professional to work with your child. You're going to have to dig deep here, either into your pocket, or with your own time and energy. This crab's blinkers are well and truly on, and you'll never prise them off, no matter how big your crowbar is.

Tip # 3: In their eyes, you're completely deluded.

In their eyes, you are just a deluded mother that went to a kibbutz somewhere in the States, hugged a few trees, and now thinks she knows everything about autism. The poor dear.

You can bet your bottom dollar that when you leave a meeting, the crabs all give a collective sigh as they shuffle their papers, tutting about *how hard it is for that poor woman, having to cope with an autistic child all by herself. Bless.* Then the subject changes to something infinitely more worth their effort, like whether Donald Trump wears a toupee, or if it's just a really bad comb-over. Let them. They don't know any better either, and you can't teach them anything because they already know it all.

Tip # 4: Write down what crabs say verbatim and watch their faces when you quote them again a few years later.

I have found that presenting the evidence in a dead-pan manner is particularly effective as it makes their incredulity and abhorrent denial even funnier. When they deny it, calmly list the date and location of their famous quotes for added authenticity, then just say nothing and await their response. Try to keep a straight face when they respond in total denial.

Tip # 5: Now you know why superheroes wear their knickers outside their tights.

No doubt your pelvic floor muscles were weakened by your pregnancy. So, consider wearing an extra pair of industrial-strength underwear when attempting Tip # 4 because if you manage to control your facial reaction, you might not be as lucky with your bladder.

Tip # 6: It's true, you do know more about your child's autism than a crab does.

And you always will. Always. Don't ever believe a crab when they try to convince you they know better. They are too far up their own arses to realise that they don't, nor do they have any idea how institutionalised they have become, or how thick they really are.

Tip # 7: A crab never admits to Tip # 6, even when it's blatantly obvious to everyone in the room.

And when they say nothing, it's because they're scared of digging an even bigger hole for themselves, so they decide to cut their losses and keep it zipped. A crab will always attempt to save face no matter what. You can present all the facts and figures you want, and they will refuse to accept them. They are entrenched in their views, and the more you try to persuade, the more polarised in their views they become.

Tip # 8: Crabs love buzzwords

A crab gets excited when it learns a new buzzword, and they are simply dying to use it on you. Let them. They'll feel so much better for it. Then gently explain why they are so very, very, wrong. I had a conversation with a crab one day that went something like this:

Crab: '. . . and Rosemary's speech needs some work, particularly in relation to her echolalia.'
Me: 'Echolalia?'
Crab: 'Yes, echolalia.'

Me: 'I'm sorry, I don't know what you are talking about. Rosemary has never engaged in any scripting or parroting back before. And you say she's doing this with you?'

Crab: 'Erm, she finds it difficult to express herself? When she tries to express herself, she can't seem to find the right words?'

Me: 'Are you referring to her word-finding difficulties, Mrs Crab?'

Crab: 'Word-finding difficulties! That's what I meant! Sorry, I just couldn't find the right word.'

Me: 'Tell me, did you eventually locate it behind the word "irony?"'

Tip # 9: Don't let a crab know how much distaste you really have for them

You need accomplices, not enemies. Take it from someone who has learned the hard way, comparing a crab to a reasonably priced car or a Disney character will never win them over.

Tip # 10: Crabs have no backbone and their brains are smaller than a pencil tip[17].

PART III

The Success

CHAPTER 17

What's the Secret?

Ring! Ring!
　　'Hello?'

'Hello, Ms Bernadette! It's Mrs Wright speaking, Rosemary's teacher.'

'Hello, Mrs Wright. Welcome back! You'd been unwell for a while, hadn't you? Are you feeling better?'

'Oh, yes, thank you, much better. It's just I thought I should call you about Rosemary.'

Oh, God! What is it now?

'I was very poorly and was off work for ten weeks, would you believe it? No, I just thought I'd call to ask you something. What's the secret?'

'The secret to my radiant complexion, Mrs Wright?'

'Well, that, too!' She chuckled. 'No, I wanted to call you about Miss Rosemary! She is a different child! A completely different child! When I went off sick, as you know, she was doing a lot better than before, but she was still struggling to control her impulses, and there were a few behaviours here and there. But, I was greeted by a mature and confident young lady in class this morning! I couldn't get over her! And her language is so much better! She tested so well today. She's at mainstream level across the board; in fact, she is a year, maybe two years, above her age in maths and spellings! I mean, we could see her gradually improving. When you're in the thick of it, you don't always notice the change, so it took for me to be out of it for a while to see the difference in her! And all in the space of ten short weeks! I had to pinch myself, Miss Bernadette! What on earth have you been doing with her? Does she suddenly have a twin I've never met? What's the secret?'

Did I just imagine that?

It's not often I'm lost for words, but I was that day.

'Em . . . well, she's been doing a bit of work for me most days after school, and . . . and had been doing Son-Ri . . . em, socialisation exercises, and stuff like that . . .', I trailed off.

'Well, I was so pleasantly surprised. I just had to call you to tell you! I am delighted for her! So delighted!'

'Em, thank you, Mrs Wright. I think she missed you when you were away. It's good that you're back.'

A bit of small talk, a little bit more gushing enthusiasm, and a couple of thank-yous later, the call ended, and I replaced the receiver.

It's all coming together now! The dream is coming true!

CHAPTER 18

By George, She's Got It!

Now tell me, how can a child with a moderate learning disability and severe language delay catch up with her mainstream peers in the space of two years? Rosemary had done so! However, on paper, she had three disabilities—autism, learning disability, and severe language delay. Maybe it was time to have her tested again.

I googled a professional testing centre and made arrangements for Rosemary to be reassessed for any learning disability. On the day I brought Rosemary in and got her settled with a book before leaving her with the assessor. I waited nervously in the café next door for a couple of hours before returning for the results of the testing.

The results? She tested at the level expected for any child her age. She had caught up academically and had a normal IQ. My daughter did not have a learning disability. I was right all along, she was not stupid. She was an intelligent young lady whose hard work had paid off.

The testing official smiled at me.

'And she's a delightful little girl, too', she added.

'Yes, she is, isn't she?' I smiled back.

Back home, I cracked my knuckles and opened her new speech and language book. So learning disability sorted, now it's time for her language deficit.

Phase 2, the Home Education Phase ended, and Phase 3, the Speech and Language Phase, commenced.

'Okay, Rosemary, who is *first* in the line?'

'The crocodile!' she beamed.

'Yes! Good girl.'

'Now tell me, who is *behind* the sheep?'

'The puppy!'

'Yes! High five!'

Slap!

'Now, who is *in front of* the last animal?'

'The lion!'

'Excellent work! You get extra playtime for working so hard today!'

I had tried to squeeze in as much speech and language work as I could as she was due for a reassessment of her language skills at school any day now. I shuddered at the memory of that fateful phone call with the speech and language therapist. After all that fuss, she delivered the sum total of two hours' worth of Speech and Language tuition, *whoop de doo*, then promptly went off on long term sick leave and wasn't replaced, so for the last two or so years, I had taken over all of her language work.

My mother used to drive a Fiat, and it never worked either.

I sat back in the chair. Rosemary's language skills had most definitely improved, but had they improved enough to lose her language delay diagnosis? There was only one way to find out.

By this time, about three years had passed since we first embarked on the Son-Rise journey, and my little Ferrari had certainly driven a very long way in a relatively short time. I had returned to full-time hours at work but had to take on a new role within the company, which made my professional working life pretty full on as well. I busied myself with work and some extra language sessions with Rosemary, waiting for her speech and language assessment.

Then the phone rang.

'Oh, hello, Miss Bernadette? It's Sarah Davies here, Rosemary's Speech and Language Therapist.'

'Oh, hi there.'

Actually, you're not her Speech and Language Therapist, I am, but I'm not going to argue with you again, not after last time. I think we could both argue at Olympic standards.

'Sorry for calling you like this, but I just couldn't wait to speak to you!'

She sounded like an excited teenager.

'I assessed Rosemary today for her language delay, and she did really well!'

Excited wasn't the word. This Fiat was gushing with enthusiasm down the phone to me. *Careful now, don't want to blow a gasket, love.*

'In fact, she's done so well I can't begin to tell you how thrilled I am! I have her results here somewhere. Now, where are they?'

I heard the frantic rustle of papers . . . again.

'Ah! Yes! Are you aware of what standardised testing is Miss Bernadette?'

'Sorry, no, I don't think so.'

'Well, the testing is based on the theory that a typical child will always score 100, no matter how easy or hard the test was. There is a standard deviation of 15, meaning that any score between 85 and 115 would be considered typical or within range, as the powers that be prefer to say. So, she was tested in the four main areas of speech, and her results are 95, 95, 97, and 98! This is excellent news! She doesn't have a language delay anymore! In fact, she is bang on the money! I am so pleased for her! I am so pleased for you! The school told me you were doing all her language work at home. Congratulations! Well done, Miss Bernadette! Well done indeed! It can take some time for the formal report to be done, but I was so excited and just wanted to tell you in person straight away!'

Okay, hit the pause button here, readers. Yes, the woman on the other end of the phone *was* Miss Davies, aka the Fiat. And no, she had not had a personality transplant, at least I don't think she had. It was the same woman, nice as pie, telling me how wonderful my daughter was and how wonderful my teaching was.

Do you remember the old mystery books you used to read as a kid, and you could decide how the plotline would pan out?

If you want to visit the abandoned gold mine, go to page 123. To interrogate Old Ma Henderson about her pick-up truck, go to page 456. To stop by the old forest shack to look for Red Neck Murphy, go to page 789. The thing that bugged me about this type of book was that no matter how hard I tried, I always ended up getting whacked. I would buy a new book, determined not to die this time, so I'd ask myself, what's the last thing I would do? Visit Old Ma Henderson? Right then, I'm-a-goin' to page 456 to interrogate her about her pesky ol' rootin-tootin truck, and as sure as eggs are eggs, the old biddy would be waiting in her rocking chair, rifle cocked, and ka-boom!

So, here goes.

If you want me to tell Miss Davies what a clapped out old banger she is, go to page X. If you want me to become all coy and say, 'Aw shucks it was all your hard work, Miss Davies', then go to page Y. If you want the truth, then go to page Z.

You want page Z?

Are you sure? Page X would be much more fun, you know? Alright then, page Z it is.

Spoilsport!

Page Z:

'Oh! So she doesn't have a language delay at all then?'

'No, not at all!'

'Oh, that's great news! Thank you for letting me know.'

'I really have to hand it to you, Miss Bernadette, you really did go over and above what any parent would do. I am thrilled for you both, just thrilled!'

There wasn't an ounce of sarcasm, no grudge, nothing. She was, as she had said, genuinely pleased for Rosemary and I. I thought back to the countless times I had practiced in my head what I would say to the Fiat when I got my chance, how I would tell her that I held down a full-time job, then did her job on top of it, and yet I never was paid an extra salary for doing all her work for her. I imagined how I would remind her of the dim prognosis she had given Rosemary, and how wrong she had been. *'I told you so, you negative old boot! Your expectations were so low you had to dig them out with a garden spade!',* I could have said.

Yes, I could have fired off plenty of not-so-subtle digs about sports cars and old jalopies, magic wands, and the whole gamut. I could have berated her for writing my daughter off as a lost cause without having met her. But, if truth be told, I didn't want to. Her excitement was genuine. If she had been any more excited, she would have spontaneously combusted. There was no malice in her, no jealousy—not a sour grape in sight. I felt no compulsion to rub any salt as there clearly was no open wound in the first place. I, in return, felt no malice towards this woman either. She was just doing the best she could with the limited resources available to her; that was all. Bloody hell! I even liked her! *Sweet Jesus! What the hell is wrong with me?*

Maybe it was me who had changed. Could I have matured a bit? Mellowed a bit? Had I become a new and improved version of me? Was I now the humble, tight-lipped, unassuming mother, who serenely went about her business?

Surely to goodness, no!

I cleared my throat and replied, 'Well, she was a model student for me, Miss Davies. She loved doing her speech and language work, and she worked very hard, she's a little grafter Miss Davies, and I'm very proud of her. Thanks for the phone call. I really appreciate you taking the time to let me know. Take care now. Bye.'

I replaced the receiver.

First, she loses her diagnosis of learning disability; then she loses her diagnosis of language delay. Well, just like crabs, success is contagious around here, too.

If you are reading this book and you are a speech and language therapist, teacher, or any education official tasked with budgeting special needs resources in schools, think about Rosemary and the thousands of other kids just like her who can achieve great things if given the chance. Don't give up on these children. Don't write them off. They only ask for one thing, a chance.

Funny, I mused to myself, I always imagined getting even with someone who hurt you would feel good. It didn't. All that guff about resentment and revenge being a dish that's best served cold is overrated. It doesn't feel good at all, actually. Just do your thing. Let the results speak for themselves. Nelson Mandela was once quoted as saying, "Resentment is like drinking poison and then hoping it will kill your enemies."[18] Well said, Mr Mandela. Well said!

Rosemary came into the kitchen and rustled about the cupboards looking for a snack while she watched television.

'What are you watching, pet?'

'*Columbo.*'

'*Columbo*? Is that still on TV these days?'

'Yeah, it's really good, you know.'

She opened the fridge and grabbed a water bottle.

'He's actually really smart', she continued.

'Who, dear?'

'Lieutenant Columbo. He only acts stupid, so the murderer thinks he's gotten away with it.'

Back into the living room, she went.

I stood for a while. That was insightful of her. I remained there at the kitchen counter, half chopped carrots on the block, and knife held aloft. Time stood still while I looked back on her journey. She had lost her diagnosis of learning disability and language delay, was doing well at school academically and socially, made friends with a best friend starting to reveal herself, and was getting invited to parties and sleepovers. She was due to transfer full time into a mainstream class the following September.

Had she done it? Had she achieved *normal* functioning, just like her peers? She was still shy, especially with new people or new situations, but it didn't take her long to come out of her shell. She still had her sunny personality that my mother begged me to preserve. I still had my Rosemary, but without the problematic behaviours she once had.

Did I dare to say it? Had she done it? Had she overcome enough of her autism difficulties as well? Had she crossed the finish line?

CHAPTER 19

Superheroes Do Exist

I could not write this book without mentioning someone who flew into my life just in time to save my world. It happened one fine summer morn, just as I was lying, wrists and ankles bound, on the railway tracks, as you do.

'Oh, somebody, please save me!', I implored as the dastardly villain tweaked his moustache and laughed his evil laugh at my predicament. 'Here comes the 10:15, right on time!', he sneered as he licked his dairy laden Mr Whippy ice cream cone with optional chopped nuts and flake for 50p extra.

I struggled to free myself, but the ropes were too tight. As the 10:15 from Stoke-on-Trent came around the corner, smoke a-billowing, horn a-whistling, a sight way up high in the sky caught my eye. Is it a bird? Is it a plane? No! It's Super Steve!

Super Steve swept down towards me, his superhero cape flowing in the jet stream.

'Fear not, fair maiden! I will free you from these train tracks, just as I liberate your previously dashed hopes and dreams for Rosemary!', he warbled as he knelt beside me, and with one almighty superhero lunge, my ropes spontaneously unravelled. He scooped me up in his overly ripped arms and flew off into the sunset with me.

'Holy guacamole! You got here just in time!', I gasped.

'I had a following wind ma'am!' came his heroic reply.

'Oh, thank you . . . erm . . . Mr . . . erm . . .?'

'My name is Super Steve! Defender of the Universe! Tra-la-la!'

That's how we met. Really! Honestly! Oh, alright then, I googled him! That's how we met. Satisfied?

I made contact with Steven when Rosemary was coming towards the end of her Son-Rise phase. What caught my attention was a statement on Steven Wertz's Growing Minds website[19]. "We can breathe new life into programs that have lost momentum." After over a year of Son-Rise work, Rosemary had plateaued because the programme had become stale and needed an injection of new energy. She was, at that stage, well within Stage 5 of the Behavioural Model, where the end was in sight, but progress had slowed to an agonising pace.

Steven had been one of the original staff members of The Son-Rise Program and was also qualified in ABA. He stated on his website that some children on the spectrum also struggle with something called executive function skills. These were skills in relation to organisation, impulse control, memory planning, attention, sustained activity, shifting between activities, initiating, emotional control, and motor control. My mouth dropped open when I read this section of the website. My daughter *did* struggle with some elements of executive function, and up until now, these skills deficits had never even been on my radar.

I made a Skype appointment with Steven and talked about Rosemary in length. He was very happy with how her Son-Rise Program was going but advised to add a series of short drills whilst sitting at the table to be interspersed between longer periods of play. Her Son-Rise play sessions would begin as normal, and about halfway through, her Son-Rise facilitator was to shout, "Okay! Table Time!" Rosemary would have to be able to sit still and pay attention long enough to complete the tasks set by Steven. When she had finished, her playtime would resume. Now Rosemary absolutely loved her Son-Rise playtime, but would she be flexible enough to stop play and pay attention to her table time? There was only one way to find out.

We tried it out the next day, and she loved it! It was a success! I could see right from the get-go that each task was designed to challenge her weaknesses in executive function, but in a fun way.

I eagerly passed my feedback onto Steven, and very soon, she had a constantly changing Table Time curriculum planned out in advance. For Rosemary, this was a welcome change to her regular Son-Rise play, and it was certainly helping her with her sustained attention and switching between activities. New Table Time games were added every week, gradually becoming more complex. Rosemary's Son-Rise Program gained momentum when Steven's add-ons were implemented, and it helped her with the skills she needed to succeed in school.

After about two years of Steven's input, Rosemary's executive functioning had improved so much that she could do the following:

1. Decide what she wanted to cook.
2. Google the recipe.
3. Copy out the recipe into her book.
4. Create a list of ingredients.
5. Check which ingredients we already had in the kitchen.
6. Create a shopping list.
7. Get a shopping bag from the cupboard.

8. Get into the car while I drove her to the supermarket.
9. Exit the car with the shopping bag and my purse.
10. Safely cross the car park.
11. Go shopping for the ingredients.
12. Pay for her items.
13. Pack her items.
14. Return to me in the car and give back my purse.

More difficult than you'd think, isn't it?

Then I would drive her home, and help her while she followed the recipe and made something for our dinner, supervised, of course. When you break down the steps just like I have done, you'll realise just how hard it is for kids with executive function difficulties.

During one Skype conversation with Steven in the earlier stages, he asked me to video Rosemary reading a book. 'I want to see what her eyes are doing', he said. After watching it back, he asked me to take Rosemary to a Behavioural Optometrist as he thought there might be a tracking issue with her eyes. He was correct in his assumption as Rosemary was found to have something called binocular vision dysfunction. A pair of glasses for six months, a few daily exercises, and a year of check-ups later, the issue was resolved. This, too, had been below my radar.

Steven even helped me prepare for IEP meetings at her new school, told me the right questions to ask, and advised me on gaining her school's co-operation with my sometimes off-the-wall suggestions about how to adapt their teaching methods. I always got so nervous before those school meetings after having my fingers so badly burnt at *that* school meeting. They never did find the fuselage.

It was Steven who picked me up and dusted me off one evening over Skype when I could barely control my tears. I poured out my woes to him about how isolated I felt, about how angry I was at so-called professionals for completely writing her off, "stealing my dreams", as I put it. I vented anger at myself for almost believing the dim prognosis given by the paediatrician, her speech and language therapist, her teacher, and acting principal at the special school. He listened to my mucous ridden blubs about how nobody understood me, about how hopeless Rosemary's future would have been if I had believed those so-called professionals. Then bit by bit, he helped me pick up the pieces. He reminded me how far Rosemary had come in such a short space of time, comparing her skills as they were to what they were before Son-Rise. He understood me. He really got me, just like the Son-Rise folk got me.

I asked Steven to add a new and refreshing element into Rosemary's Son-Rise Program, and he did just that and so much more. He was there with Rosemary and me every single step of the way, always excited to hear our news, and his celebrations at her mini successes along the way were genuine. Superheroes are supposed to save the world, but Super Steve saved me from myself. He stood beside me at the cliff edge of my sanity and coaxed me back to safety. If it wasn't for Super Steve, Defender of the Universe, I would have jumped.

CHAPTER 20

Super Kid Training Without Breaking the Bank

As a keen Facebook group member, website follower, and general googler of all things autism-related, it never ceases to amaze me just how expensive some autism interventions can be. Many parents spend in excess of $15,000 annually[20] (about £12,000[21]) on treatments and programmes. £12,000 annually! Who has that kind of money? When I added up how much I have spent for Rosemary's entire five-year programme, including Son-Rise, home-school, speech and language, executive functioning, I estimated it to be somewhere in the region of £16,000 total. That's a big difference! And because Son-Rise is parent-led and run, I did not have to pay a professionally qualified therapist to work one on one with

Rosemary full time as some other intervention programmes require.

Still, £16,000 is a lot of money if you are a single mother who works as a secretary, especially when your shopping trolley is laden with organic, dairy-free, gluten-free, corn-free soy-free, low-sugar food. But somehow, I made it work. Okay, maybe I was walking around with holes in my tee-shirt, my shoes let in water and squeaked when I walked in the rain, and yes, I did look an absolute fright, but it was worth every single penny saved.

I paid in other ways, too. I paid with my physical and mental health. I thought I was being financially savvy, splurging on Rosemary's food, and grabbing anything cheap and cheerful for myself. While Rosemary ate well, I ate sugar-laden junk and way too much of it. That's what calmed me. That's what pushed my feelings back down to the pit of my stomach and kept them there. Slowly but surely, I ate my way up to over fifteen stones. I was a ticking time bomb.

Nobody ever tells you how stressful raising a child can be, and it is double when raising a special child. Going against the crowd and actively helping your child overcome their disabilities isolates you even further, raising the stress levels some more. Try and hold down a job at the same time, and the stress levels keep going up. Oh, yeah, and I got bullied at work for a year during that time, so more stress, and let's not forget single motherhood. With my lifestyle as it was, I had created the perfect storm, and I was headed straight for the eye of it.

I knew what I needed to do:

1. Eat healthily.
2. Exercise.
3. Do something just for me at least once a week.
4. Get into mindfulness/yoga/EFT/meditation/ aromatherapy.
5. Get a good life coach.

Did I do any of these? Hell no! Well, not during Rosemary's treatment years anyway. It was really after I realised that Rosemary had surpassed all the dreams I had for her when I finally accepted that she really and truly had done it, did I turn the focus on myself. I should have done it sooner. Have a look at that list again. It looks expensive, doesn't it? Gym membership, yoga classes, EFT people, and life coaches are expensive. Tell me, just how many life coaches out there are going to identify with an autism mum's unique situation and journey? How many of them are closet crabs, telling you to believe what the paediatrician said about your daughter possibly requiring institutionalisation? Well, if the mountain will not come to Mohammed and all that jazz . . .

My mind was made up. I studied EFT (Emotional Freedom Technique or tapping) and became an accredited EFT therapist. I also became a life coach and studied mindfulness, meditation, and aromatherapy. I eat healthily and exercise every day, and it cost me a fraction of what it would have cost, had I paid for the services of a life coach.

Now I help rookie super mums, and super dads do what I should have done from the start, take care of themselves properly. You can't have the three E's (energy, excitement, and enthusiasm) if you are a bundle of nerves. Our special kids are sensitive souls who can pick up on the tiniest detail. When you are stressed, they are stressed. When you are uptight, they feel it, too. You can't raise a calm and measured child if you are a train wreck yourself. Get your stress levels under control, look after you, and I promise you, helping your super kid unleash their superpowers will be much easier.

When I work with my clients, I encourage them to use their newly learned skills on their children, too. A client of mine in India adapted her EFT (tapping therapy) for her son, who used it when he felt anxious about school, and it really worked.

One thing I promise all my clients when providing them with life coaching sessions is that there are some things that I will never say to them:

1. You should give up on your dreams for yourself and your child.
2. You are harming your child.
3. You're no expert.
4. Listen to the paediatricians, teachers, and therapists when they say your child will never achieve any semblance of a *normal* life because they know best.
5. Resign yourself to the fact that your child will probably have to be institutionalised.

I have cried with them, laughed with them, and celebrated every milestone with them. Finally, there is a proper job for a super mum like me, and that is to assist newbie superheroes through their superhero cadet training. To cheer as they turn their special kids into super kids, and of course, to save the universe before it's time for gluten and dairy-free dinner.

As you move towards the end of your Son-Rise Program, or your home-school programme, or your speech and language programme, or even your executive functioning skills programme, you will probably still find that your super kid may still need to be taught skills that neurotypicals seem to just pick up along the way. I soon learned that I needed to *drill the skill*, as I liked to say. Neurotypicals take a lot of things for granted and fail to understand just how complicated some tasks really are. For instance, going swimming seems like an easy uncomplicated Saturday morning activity, right? Wrong! Here's what you need to do to go swimming:

1. Decide if you are going to wear your underwear or swimwear, to begin with.
2. Decided on the latter? Okay, then you need to pack underwear.
3. Now pack everything else: goggles, towel, shampoo, conditioner, soap or shower gel, comb, money or card to pay for swim session, plus £1 coin for the locker, plus a 20p coin for the hairdryer and your purse.
4. Go to the swimming pool.
5. Go to the changing rooms.
6. Take all your outside clothes off and put all your belongings in the locker.
7. Arrange your belongings in the locker so you can easily grab your towel, shampoo, conditioner, soap or shower gel, and comb when you are wet from the pool.
8. Put the £1 coin in and lock the locker.
9. Put the key wristband on your nondominant wrist and close it properly (it's harder than it sounds).
10. Remember your locker number.
11. Go swimming.
12. Watch out/listen out for when it's time to leave the pool.
13. Finish swimming and come back to your locker.
14. Take off key-wristband, unlock your locker, and grab what you need to go to the shower.

15. Retrieve £1 from the bottom of the lock, reinsert, and lock the locker again.
16. Remember to bring the key-wrist band to the showers with you.
17. Wash your body, wash and condition your hair, and rinse well.
18. Dry yourself.
19. Towel dry and comb your hair.
20. Collect your shampoo, conditioner bottles, and your soap or shower gel.
21. Return to your locker and unlock it.
22. Remove everything from the locker and take into the changing room with you.
23. Retrieve £1 from the bottom of the locker and put it in your purse.
24. Get changed into your outdoor clothes.
25. Put your shoes on.
26. Put all your belongings, except your bikini and towel, into your bag.
27. Put your bikini in the dryer and spin for a few seconds.
28. Tear off a disposable wet garments bag and place your bikini and towel inside.
29. Dry your hair with the hairdryer using the 20p you brought.
30. Bring your bag and disposable bag with you and go to the spot in the leisure centre where your mum said she would meet you.

Doesn't seem so simple now, does it? It took Rosemary a few attempts with me running in and out of the changing rooms to help her along, but each week I faded my prompts. Once they get the skill, they will retain it.

I remember when she was younger and was scared of hand dryers in public bathrooms. I would always let her dry her hands using a paper towel instead, and I would do likewise. But inevitably, I would see out of the corner of my eye somebody approaching the dryer. Everything would go into slow motion as she stretched her hands outwards.

No! Don't do it! Don't use the hand dryer!

The hand dryer would whoosh into action, Rosemary would scream and cover her ears, and I would usher her out as quickly as I could, trying to pacify a frightened little girl. I'm sure many of you are familiar with this scenario. I knew there was going to be only one thing for it, and I was going to have to drill the skill. I rang the shopping mall and asked if we could visit when there were no shoppers there. The shopping mall manager was accommodating and made arrangements for us to come early one Sunday morning. We were met at the front door by Laura, who let us go into the bathrooms and start our Son-Rise play there. (This, too, occurred during Rosemary's Son-Rise phase). Believe it or not, but when we were having a picnic on the moon, as we very frequently did in Son-Rise world, a brisk and refreshing breeze swept over the arid landscape.

Whoosh!

'Thanks, Laura!'

'No problem, Ruthangela!'

'Oh, my goodness, Rosemary! How on earth are we going to move all this moon dust over to Barbie's moon mansion? She needs to give the moon dust to the fairies at the bottom of her moon garden! If only we could just blow it over!'

'I know mummy! I get the winds to blowed it!'

'Great idea, Rosemary!'

Little Miss Madam tiptoed over to the hand dryer and *whoosh*!

By the end of the two-hour session, Laura was getting a cut and blow-dry at *Rosemary's Lovely Hair Salon*. Suffice to say she ended up looking windswept and interesting.

Drilling the skill needs little or no money to do. The less you help your child, the more you help them. By that, I mean let them tie their own shoelaces and button their own shirts. If they want a cake in the café (gluten and dairy-free, of course), then they have to approach the counter, wait to be served, look at the server, ask for it, pay for it, and bring it back to the table. Mums instinctively do things for their children without thinking. Stop it. Hang back and let them do it themselves. You will be doing them a favour. Five years on, Laura still stops Rosemary for a chat every time we go shopping.

Rosemary had popped into the supermarket for her recipe ingredients one Saturday while I stayed in the café finishing off my drink.

'Ruthangela! How's it going?'

I looked up from my cuppa and newspaper. It was Carole, the mum of one of Rosemary's school friends.

'Oh, hi, Carole, how are things?'

'Where's Rosemary?'

'Just running around the supermarket getting a few ingredients for dinner tonight.'

'What? She cooks for you both?'

'Yeah, once a week.'

'And she's okay in the shop by herself?'

'Oh, yes, she's fine. She's got her phone with her if she needs me. Didn't little Eleanor fancy the school trip then?'

'No, she didn't want to go. She didn't want to spend a week away from me. She's still so clingy, you know, I don't know what to do.'

'Oh, she'll grow out of it, I'm sure', I assured her.

'So what's The Screamer making for you tonight then?'

'Sorry? What?'

'The Screamer? That's what they used to call her at the special school.'

'The Screamer? No, it was The Runner, and that was at nursery.'

'Don't you remember I used to be a dinner lady at the special school? No, they definitely called her The Screamer, because she used to run through the corridors screaming her head off! She was absolutely petrified, the little darling. She's come a long way since then, hasn't she?'

So it would appear that whatever happened in the special school, stayed in the special school. I suppose that would explain the box of 24 loaves of gluten-free bread for the freezer I delivered to their reception desk that they never received. I never did get to the bottom of why the teacher ripped the hood of Rosemary's coat when she tried to grab Rosemary by the scruff of her neck "completely by accident, of course," one day. That teacher, who incidentally was never named, must have had near on superhero strength to rip the hood clear off. They apparently also had a nickname for her that they did not care to share with me, nor did they consider it relevant that my daughter was so traumatised by them that she tried to escape out of pure terror.

I took a deep breath and said, 'She's making chicken curry tonight.'

'I wish that my Eleanor was more like Rosemary. Eleanor won't go to sleepovers even for one night, never mind the whole week with the school to France! And there's your Rosemary, going shopping by herself and doing the cooking!'

'And cleaning!', I interjected. 'She cleans the house for me every weekend for her pocket money.'

'You know, Eleanor needs to spend more time with Rosemary. Some of Rosemary's common sense might rub off on her.'

Her phone beeped. She looked at it.

'I'd better get going, that's Eleanor wanting to know when I'll be home. She'll only let her dad or her grandma look after her, and even then, she's counting down the minutes until I get back. Must dash. Call me?'

Carole whirled out of the shopping centre just as quickly as she had whirled in. I spotted Rosemary with her bagful of shopping and waved to her. I watched as she lugged the shopping bag over towards me, smiling.

What was it that Carole had said? "I wish that my Eleanor was more like Rosemary." Eleanor, her eleven-year-old daughter, who was in the same class as Rosemary, and had no diagnoses of any description. Eleanor never had an IEP or a classroom assistant in all her born days and got mostly C's in her end of year report, when Rosemary got mostly B's.

Eleanor didn't like being without her mum. I could leave Rosemary on her own in the house for a couple of hours, with no reservations. Rosemary would have no qualms if I left her all day by herself, but I wasn't prepared to do that. After all, she was only eleven.

On weekdays, I leave the house to go to work before she does. She waits at home for the school bus, lets herself out of the house, locks the door, and makes her way to school. She also lets herself into the house when the bus brings her back in the afternoon, she makes herself a snack, and starts her homework before I arrive home.

She has friends and goes to parties and sleepovers. She even went on a school trip to France for an entire week. She was now in a regular mainstream class, in a regular mainstream school, and she was thriving.

Gone were all her previous stims, previous obsessions, her repetitive speech was no more, and she had great eye contact. She was also flexible in her interactions. In fact, to the untrained eye, she was a typical eleven-year-old girl.

I cast my mind back to what the paediatrician told me on diagnosis day.

". . . She may well be able to cope in adulthood if she were to secure a place in a supported living environment, which, of course, would be preferable to placing her in full-time care."

I thought of Patsy's son, Oliver, who had graduated from The Son-Rise Program and blended in with all the other boys his age in school. I thought of Lou at the breakfast table in America and how he inspired me to work with my daughter so that, someday, she may be capable of looking after herself in the world. Some day? How about now? Rosemary was eleven and could fend for herself better than most kids her age.

Had she done it? Had she overcome her autism difficulties? I looked at my daughter's beautiful face and smiled.

'Let me take that bag for you, dear. Got everything?'

We walked to the car and loaded up the boot.

So, was Rosemary still autistic? Yes, a few bits of autism remained, just like with Oliver and Lou. Most of the time, Rosemary behaved like any neurotypical child, but she was uber-sensitive to stress and perseverated on problems. She had friends, but she wasn't a social butterfly. That was the negative part. The good part about Rosemary's autism was that she did not have a single ounce of nastiness in her entire body. She was as beautiful on the inside as she was on the outside. She is the first pupil in her class to feel sorry for another kid who is having a hard time. She is the first to forgive, and last to bear a grudge.

She is a sensitive and beautiful soul. She is unique.

I have a lot to thank autism for.

CHAPTER 21

Top of the Class

I stand in the office while I wait. This morning's workout was harder than I thought, my leg muscles are still burning, but it's worth it, being a stone lighter already.

I glance up at the picture of the smiling salmon fisher on the wall as the clock ticks. Rosemary is being assessed for her comprehension and mathematics skills at the Top of the Class. I wonder if the assessor recognises us from before. He appears at the door and hands me a sheet of A4 paper, his moustache moving to reveal a smile underneath. Today, his black moustache is peppered with a few greys.

'Just a basic form for all new students', he explains. 'I have one for every child. What is it exactly that you need me to do for Rosemary?'

'Oh, I just wanted to keep the old brain ticking over the summer holidays, that's all.'

'Ah, yes, indeed, you'll be amazed how much they forget over the summer, and it all has to be relearned again in September. I was wondering actually what you wanted me to do for her. She's clearly a very capable and intelligent young lady. She'll have a good head start on her classmates by September then.'

I bend my head to look at the form, hiding my secret smile. I start filling out the boxes.

He stands over me for a moment. 'Erm . . . actually, you look awfully familiar. Have we met before?'

I stop writing and look up.

'I'm not sure, have we?'

Silence. We look at each other.

'Oh! She needs a homework folder. I almost forgot. Now, where did I put them?' he busies himself gathering together some worksheets for Rosemary and I sign the form.

We leave the Top of the Class offices and get in the car. I turn to my beautiful daughter and smile.

'Whack the radio up, will you love?'

We stop at the lights. I open the window to get some air circulating. The guy in the car next to us shoots us a disapproving glance as the beats of "Barbie Girl" by Aqua [22] pump from the car stereo.

"Come on, Barbie, let's go party!"

The lights turn green, and I flash him a smile and a wink as we drive away.

Cheeky? Moi?

PART IV

The Secrets

CHAPTER 22

The 10 Secrets of Unleashing Your Child's Superpowers

Hey, Ruthangela, it's your future self here. How's it going? I bet you're wondering why I've contacted you out of the blue like this. Well, it's pretty simple, you sent me. Your future self wanted you to know a few things that you really weren't supposed to learn for another ten years or so.

So, here I am!

You know you're a super mum, don't you? Don't look at me like that! Yes, you are a super mum, and you are going to help other super mums and super dads who are super-stuck right now, just like you were stuck for the longest time.

Do you know you helped your child overcome autism difficulties? Well, you did. And not just autism, but a learning disability and language delay, too. Oh, sorry! Am I going too fast for you? Yes, that's right, your beautiful baby girl sleeping in her cot right now will receive diagnoses of autism, learning disability, and language delay. But don't panic, it's okay because you're going to unleash your super kid's superpowers. Yeah, she's a superhero, too.

But I'm getting ahead of myself here. Is that the time already? Right then, let's get to work. I haven't got all day, you know. Now grab a pen. I'm going to give you *The 10 Secrets of Unleashing Your Child's Superpowers*.

Secret #1: The Ultimate Secret

By far, the most important secret. Remember it and remember it well.

You and you alone are the expert on your child. Nobody else knows more about your kid than you do. Oh, some may think they are more knowledgeable about your child, but they are deluding themselves because they don't. And get this . . . they are the ones who will say that *you* are the deluded one.

By no means am I suggesting you forge ahead with your mission without listening to experts in their fields. Yes, you are the expert on your child as a whole, but you need to listen to doctors, speech and language therapists, occupational therapists, teachers, etc. sometimes. Ultimately, it is up to you what you do with their advice. You and only you can make that choice because you are the expert.

Secret #2: Listen to Your Gut

Remember the old saying, "Mother knows best?" It's true. When it comes to your kid, you *do* know best. Your gut will tell you if something isn't right. It doesn't lie. Sorry dads, but when God was handing out gut instincts, he missed most of you.

Secret # 3: Ignore Ignore Ignore

Ignore the crabs. Ignore the naysayers. Ignore the well-meaners. Ignore the expectation- managers. These sorts are particularly adept at grabbing you with their pincers and dragging you back down into the bucket. Don't let them drag you down. You've got work to do, and you need to get out of that bucket to do it. So, ignore these people, but never *ever* ignore your gut.

Secret # 4: Your child is a sensitive soul

Your child picks up on every nuance, inference, hint of annoyance/impatience/joy/excitement in your voice and mannerisms. Autism does not equal stupid, and just because some of them can't speak, or express themselves eloquently, does not mean they don't understand what is going on. They do. They get it. In fact, they are so intuitive that they appreciate what is going on in a much deeper way than you can even contemplate. If you are stressed, they feel it. If you are depressed, they feel it. Never ever talk about your child in front of them. Choose your words, tone, and body language carefully, and tell others to do likewise.

Secret # 5: Start Early

You should have started earlier. When I say earlier, I mean like when she was eighteen months old, not six-and-a-half. If you had started then, it would have been much easier, it would have taken considerably less time, and you could have saved yourself a whole lot of heartache. But hey, you got there in the end, didn't you? Nobody needs a diagnosis of any kind to start Son-Rise.

Secret # 6: Choose a school like you would choose a spouse

Yep, it's that important. And let's face it, seven or eight years in any school is a longer time than a lot of marriages these days. I would have preferred it if you had taken her out of school completely and "Son-Rised" and home-schooled her yourself for a couple of years, because you would have covered much more ground in a shorter space of time if you had. But, you couldn't afford to do that, and you needed to work to bring home the bacon, so I respect your decision to do it the way you did. When choosing your child's school, listen to your gut.

Secret # 7: Dig Deep

You will spend a lot of money. There is no way around this fact. You will have to dig deep into your pockets and deep within yourself to resource this project. Choose what you spend your money on wisely. Some parents have taken out a second mortgage on their home to fund their kid's interventions, but you won't need to take such drastic action. You won't realise it at the time, but you chose the most cost-effective way of helping Rosemary.

Secret # 8: This will isolate you

You will lose friends. You will lose acquaintances. You and your child will be marooned upon Son-Rise-Home-school Island for a few years, but that's alright because the view from the top of Son-Rise-Home-school Mountain far outweighs the climb. But you could do without any extra baggage along the way.

You will also lose the respect of many people, because in their eyes, you are that idiotic woman who went to that hippie place in the States, banged a drum, and ate a few magic mushrooms. Let them think whatever they want because what they think is none of your business.

Secret # 9: Make allies, not enemies

You're in for a marathon, not a sprint here, and the more support you can find, the better. Don't lose your temper with people who honestly believe they are helping you, even if they're not. Don't shoot your mouth off at them and burn your bridges, even if they do deserve it.

Newsflash! Not all teachers/therapists/clinicians care about your kid. Sorry to have to break it to you, but it's true. You'll be able to spot them quite easily. They're the ones who might look like they are listening to you when really they're just waiting for their turn to talk. They don't know any better, so go easy on them. Not all of them are as bad as that, and some of them are really talented. So, do me a favour, will you? Squeeze out a semblance of civility with these people every now and again? Please?

Secret # 10: Look after you

Take it from me, Ruthangela, you might have helped Rosemary, but you almost killed yourself in the process. Looking after yourself is just as important as looking after your special child. If you are running on empty, it will show in your work with your child, and you will lack the 3 Es.

Remember the safety drill on board the plane. 'If travelling with a child, always attend to your own oxygen mask before securing theirs.' If you can't find a good life coach, someone who understands the unique work that you are doing, then become a life coach yourself.

What are you looking at me like that for Ruthangela? I'm only doing what you asked me to. Lord knows I don't have much time to spare these days.

Right then! Have you got all that? I hope you remember these secrets, especially the ones about keeping a lid on your hot temper and looking after yourself. You will won't you?

Well, that's everything, I think. Got to go. See you in about ten years! Any questions?

My younger self stared at my older self in stunned silence.

Ruthangela, you need a really long break girl.

Righty-ho! Got to fly. Got an important work conference to get to because I'm Head of Sales for Mattel now, but that's just my day job, I've got to save the world first.

Has anyone seen my cape?

Acknowledgements

My sincere thanks goes to everyone at Author Academy Elite. I could never have completed this book without your help.

To my parents, for being cool with me writing about them. You supported me every step of the way with Rosemary. Thank you for believing in us.

To Steven R. Wertz, drying my tears was never part of the gig, but you did it anyway.

To everyone at The Autism Treatment Center of America: You gave me hope. You reignited the spark within me.

Appendix

[1] "Hello", Lionel Richie, *Can't Slow Down*, Motown Records, 1983

[2] "I Just Don't Know What To Do With Myself", Dusty Springfield, *Dusty*, Philips Records,1964

[3] "Keep calm and carry on" University of London, https://london.ac.uk/about-us/history-university-london/story-behind-keep-calm-and-carry, accessed 11 September 2019

[4] "Escape", Rupert Holmes, *Partners In Crime*, Infinity Records, 1979

[5] Margo Maine, Ph.D., *Body Wars*, (Carlsbad, California: Gürze Books, 2011)

[6] "Runnin' (Lose It All)", Naughty Boy, featuring artists Beyoncé and Arrow Benjamin, *Bungee Jumping*, Virgin EMI Records, 2015

[7] David Walliams, *Mr Stink*, (London: Harper Collins Publishers Ltd., 2009)

[8] "TEACCH", National Autistic Society, https://www.autism.org.uk/about/strategies/teacch.aspx, accessed 1 October 2019

[9] "What is autism", Ambitious About Autism, https://www.ambitiousaboutautism.org.uk/understanding-autism/about-autism/what-is-autism, accessed 14 September 2019

10 The Autism Treatment Center of America, https:// autismtreatmentcenter.org/, accessed 1 October 2019

11 Barry Neil Kaufman, *A Miracle To Believe In*, (New York: Doubleday & Company, 1981)

12 Barry Neil Kaufman, *Son-Rise The Miracle Continues*, (Novato, California: New World Library, 1994)

13 Barry Neil Kaufman, "Son-Rise: A Miracle Of Love", IMDb, https://www.imdb.com/title/tt0079933/?ref_ =nv_ sr_4?ref_=nv_sr_4

14 "Monty Python's Camp Military Drill", YouTube video, 0:44, posted by Henry Davies, on 1 December 2011, https://www. youtube.com/watch?v=7-2jLLMdEBw

15 "Copacabana", Barry Manilow, *Even Now*, Arista Records, 1978

16 "Crab Mentality", *Wikipedia*, https://en.wikipedia.org/wiki/ Crab_mentality, accessed 11 September 2019

17 "How Can Crabs Move If All They Have Inside Is Pure Meat", *Quora*, https://www.quora.com/How-can-crabs-move-if-al l-they-have-inside-is-pure-meat, accessed 11 September 2019

18 "Nelson Mandela Transformed Himself And Then His Nation", *Los Angeles Times*, https://www.latimes.com/opinion/ topoftheticket/la-xpm-2013-dec-06-la-na-tt-nelson-mande la-20131206-story.html, accessed 14 September 2019

19 "Growing Minds Autism Programs", https://www. autism-programs.com/index.htm, accessed 11 September 2019

20 "Parents Of Autistic Children Fight For Treatment In An Unforgiving Market", *The Guardian*, https:// www.theguardian.com/money/2014/apr/21/ autism-children-parents-therapy-insurance-treatment, accessed 14 September 2019

21 "XE Currency Converter", https://www.xe.com, accessed 17 October 2019

22 "Barbie Girl", Aqua, *Aquarium*, MCA Records, 1997

About the Author

Ruthangela Bernadette turned her special kid into a super kid. Her passion is to inspire and empower parents to do likewise. She is a public speaker and life coach, but that's just her day job, her real job is raising her eye-rolling, door slamming, make-up wearing, super teen daughter, and of course saving the universe before dinner time.

Find out more at RuthangelaBernadette.com.

Wanna Be a Superhero, Too?

Launch yourself and your super kid into hyperspace at
RuthangelaBernadette.com

Useful Websites

Behavioural Therapy: The Autism Treatment Center of America
www.autismtreatmentcenter.org

Growing Minds Autism Programs
www.autism-programs.com

Healthy Eating: Nature Doc Clinic
www.naturedoc.co.uk

Books: Autism Breakthrough
by Raun K. Kaufman

Autistic Logistics
by Kate C. Wilde

The Autism Language Launcher
by Kate C. Wilde

Play to Grow
by Tali F Berman & Abby Rappaport

The Good Stuff
Delicious Recipes and Tips
by Lucinda Miller

Achieving Speech & Language Targets
by Catherine Delamain & Jill Spring

Reading Between the Lines
by Catherine Delamain & Jill Spring

Working Memory Activities
by David Newman

Inference Activities
by David Newman

Auditory Processing of Higher-Level
Language Skills
by Jean Gillam DeGaetano

Smart But Scattered
by Peg Dawson & Richard Guare

Oxford Reading Tree
Songbirds Phonics Collection
by Julia Donaldson

CPSIA information can be obtained
at www.ICGtesting.com
Printed in the USA
LVHW101022240220
647928LV00007BA/100/J

9 781647 460631